LEADERSHIP SKILLS IN EDUCATION MANAGEMENT SERIES

Series Editor: Professor Trevor Kerry

Other titles in this series

Mastering Deputy Headship   Professor Trevor Kerry
This practical book sets out to not only identify but address the issues facing newly appointed deputies and also those who are aspiring to become a deputy head. It aims to examine the generic skills needed within such a role.

The Special Educational Needs Coordinator   Vic Shuttleworth
This practical book enables aspiring or newly appointed SENCOs (Special Educational Needs Coordinators) to approach a range of management tasks with the right knowledge and techniques to work systematically and effectively with colleagues, benefiting the most vulnerable pupils and cutting through the layers of bureaucracy to expose the bigger issues.

From Teacher to Middle Manager   Susan Tranter
This book is a practical guide aimed at busy career teachers. It explores the issues surrounding the transition from junior management to a school leadership role, describing the process of getting a post, the first few months in post and the skills required in middle management. It also looks ahead at further professional development.

For further information,
telephone Pearson Education Ltd
on 01704 508080.

The Head Teacher
in the 21ˢᵗ Century

Being a successful school leader

Frank Green

Pearson
Education

For Kate, Justin, Tom and Sam

PEARSON EDUCATION LIMITED

Head Office:
Edinburgh Gate
Harlow CM20 2JE
Tel: +44 (0)1279 623623
Fax: +44 (0)1279 431059

London Office:
128 Long Acre
London WC2E 9AN
Tel: +44 (0)20 7447 2000
Fax: +44 (0)20 7240 5771
Website: www.educationminds.com

First published in Great Britain in 2000

ISBN 0 273 65096 3

British Library Cataloguing in Publication Data
A CIP catalogue record for this book can be obtained from the British Library.

10 9 8 7 6 5 4 3 2 1

Typeset by Boyd Elliott Typesetting
Printed and bound in Great Britain by Redwood Books Ltd, Trowbridge, Wilts.

The Publishers' policy is to use paper manufactured from sustainable forests.

About the author

FRANK GREEN is Principal and Chief Executive of The Leigh City Technology College, Dartford, a post he has held for three years. Prior to that he was the founding Head of the Lincoln School of Science and Technology, which opened in 1992. His first degree is in metallurgical engineering from Imperial College.

As Principal of The Leigh CTC, he is also Chairman of their trading company and Chairman of North West Kent Teacher Trainers, a school-based initial teacher-training scheme of seven local schools. He is also a non-executive Director of Ed+, an Educational Management Services company.

Frank's main interest is in using the power of technology to transform education. He has supported and worked with the Technology College's Trust since 1992, being a member of its Council from 1995–97. In 1996 with a group of Heads from other specialist schools affiliated to the TC Trust, they set up Vision 2020, a think tank which aims to discuss, plan and implement the changes needed to make the future of education.

He has had a long involvement with business links that began in 1984. For eight years he was director of the Hove Insight into Industry scheme, a unique three-year programme for students from all the Hove secondary schools, a forerunner of many of the problem-solving industry link schemes in use today. Since 1984 Frank has been involved with Young Enterprise, having been on Area and Strategic Boards in three counties. He was Chairman of the Brighton Area from 1991–92. He has written a number of articles on education industry links and on other educational matters.

The Ofsted inspection of The Lincoln School of Science and Technology stated that it was 'a very good school, with outstanding leadership from the head.' Its first results in 1997 made it the best comprehensive school in Lincolnshire. The Leigh City Technology College has been among the ten most improved schools in the country according to the Department for Education and Employment's figures.

Contents

Series editor's introduction

The nature of schools and the educative process is changing. Indications are that the first decade of the twenty-first century will see the fastest, and the most far-reaching, changes in schools and schooling since the compulsory education system was established. The signs are there if we have eyes to see them:

- advances in technology will alter the nature of learning. While school has been characterised by the need for groups of people to assemble together to listen to a teacher, the computer, its software and the Internet are making learning accessible to anyone, according to need and inclination, without their having to come together;

- technology, through the computer and through video-conferencing, gives access on a local level to global opportunities. If they have the technology, pupils in Britain can access the very best lessons and the very best teachers from anywhere in the world. In place of thousands of teachers teaching thousands of different, more or less good, lessons on a topic, the student will be able to access the most complete and dynamic lesson regardless of where it is taught;

- computers even threaten the concept of school time. Since the computer gives access at unlimited times and in unlimited places, learning need no longer be associated with time slots at all;

- but it is not just computers that are driving the forces of education into new channels. Economics plays a part. School buildings are inflexible and costly, yet they often remain unused for more than 80 per cent of the time – during vacations, evenings, nights and so on. Costly plant lying idle is a luxury that society may feel unable to afford;

- increasingly, we can see non-teachers of various kinds becoming more central to the education process. There was a time when no adult but a teacher would have been found in a classroom. Now schools often have a greater complement of technicians, administrators, nursery assistants, special needs assistants, students from care courses, voluntary helpers and counsellors than they do of teaching staff.

So key areas – how learning takes place, where it takes place, when, its quality, the type of plant required, the nature of the people who deliver it – are all in the melting pot as we enter the new millennium. If ever there was a moment for developing a new breed of educational leaders who could span the effective management of the present system and forge a path into the future, this is it.

This series is therefore dedicated to achieving those ends: to help education managers at various levels in the system to become the leaders now and the pioneers of the future. The titles are all written by people with proven track records of innovation. The style is intended to be direct, and the reader is asked to engage with the text in order to maximise the training benefit that the books can deliver.

Change is rarely comfortable, but it can be exciting. This series hopes to communicate to school leaders something of the confidence that is needed to manage change, and something of the fulfilment that comes from meeting challenge successfully.

Professor Trevor Kerry

List of tasks

List of tables

List of figures

Preface

What drew me to write this text as part of a series of self teaching manuals on leadership in schools was that any expertise and skills that I have acquired should be available to a wider audience in case there is anything of value to others. David Hargreaves has suggested that teaching should copy the apprentice model approach used in the medical profession to transmit knowledge: that is that new or inexperienced Heads should work alongside experienced ones and learn from them. So when the opportunity was presented to tell others about the skills and expertise required of Heads I was encouraged to put my thoughts onto paper.

They are a collection of thoughts and ideas about the skills for being a Head that seem to me to be required regularly.

They make no pretensions to being comprehensive in their coverage; I have concentrated on the skills that are most important today. I have not emphasised the basic principles of headship which are exactly the same as those of any good teacher. It is assumed that the techniques of maintaining good order, discipline and good manners are known and valued by all Heads and aspiring Heads.

The nature of headship – and, therefore, leadership – of schools is rapidly changing, and the purpose of this text is to try to provide a little help to existing and aspiring leaders to find their own way down a difficult path.

It may also help others in the profession and hopefully in the wider community to understand what is going on in our schools. If it manages to achieve any of these goals it will have done as much as could be expected.

After eight years of being Head in two schools, I do not claim to be an authority on what makes a successful Head, but I can give a perspective on what I have needed to think about, do, reflect on and seek advice on during the that time. I have had the opportunity in preparing this book of talking and working with some outstanding colleagues, leaders of both primary and secondary schools. Many of them may not know it, but I always find some nugget of advice or information in every meeting with them. I go into those meetings looking for information that might be of use. I have so often picked up the phone and rung a colleague about some problem that was niggling me and to which I could not easily find a solution. The discussion that followed not only helped identify good solutions to the problem but also ways of implementing them. It is almost always true that nothing is ever entirely new in life and you can usually find someone somewhere who has met either the problem you are grappling with or one very similar. Talking to them about how they resolved it may give you enough clues to find a solution to your problem. However, it is never good enough to find any solution, you always have to ask yourself, 'Is this the best way so solve this particular problem, is there a better way?'

Acknowledgements

There are many people who have helped make this book possible. All the Heads who have been involved at any time in the last four years with Vision 2020 are owed a particular debt of gratitude, more especially those who participated in the conference in May and June 2000. I also owe a great deal to the senior staff who have worked for me in the last eight years, particularly, Dan Moynihan, Paul Watson, Brian Cartwright and Tony Downing who put up with my idiosyncrasies and helped me to become a leader of successful schools. I leave others to judge whether this makes me a successful Head.

The paper from the Vision 2020 conference is reproduced here by kind permission of the Technology Colleges Trust. The paper was created by the hard work of over 100 Heads during our three days of meetings in May and June.

The paper on the future of LEAs is reproduced by kind permission of the author, Liz Allen, who wrote it as a discussion document for the New Local Government Network.

Finally, and most importantly I must acknowledge the support of my wife, Kate, whose encouragement and persistence has, more than anything, enabled me to complete this book.

How to use this book

This book contains a great deal of knowledge in what is a rather random form. It is about some of the skills and attributes required of a Head in a primary or secondary school. At no stage would it claim to be a work of scholarship but is designed to offer a selection of some of the most effective strategies and approaches to the job of headship as it is today. The examples are mostly taken from the secondary sector as this is where my experience lies. The book uses a variety of means to set out, examine and exemplify these skills:

- text – to provide information, discussion and continuity
- tables and figures – to convey data quickly or in graphic form
- lists – to set out key issues and skills
- tasks – to involve the reader in practice
- case studies – to provide real examples of leadership/management situations.

The book can be used in a variety of ways. It can be read as a textbook: the reader will then simply read over, but not carry out, the tasks. It can be used as a source book: you can consult the relevant sections (such as creating a learning culture or financial management) as the need arises. It can be used as a training manual by an individual, in which case you will work through it systematically, pausing to carry out each task as you come to it. The book can also be used as a training manual for a course on the changing role of the Head. Finally the book can be used in conjunction with the author who will be pleased to act as an on-line trainer or mentor for aspiring or practising Heads. To get the most from the book, we recommend that you use the tasks and keep a log of the outcomes from them.

The book is based on the philosophy that effective leaders need specific skills for the job. These skills can be identified, analysed, refined, broken down into subskills, taught, learned and even assessed. We hope that the book will be seen by busy Heads and aspiring deputies as a kind of *vade-mecum* – a source of comfort and inspiration. It would be useful, too, as the basis of a systematic dialogue between a deputy or a Head and their mentor, particularly if they are on the National Professional Qualification for Headship (NPQH) or Leadership Programme for Serving Headteachers (LPSH) programme.

The book stresses the importance of the links between the practice of being a Head and the appropriate management theory that underpins specific aspects of the role. We believe that practice without theory is a house built on sand; and that theory without translation into sound practice is an empty vessel.

We trust that this manual of skills, based on grounded theory and experience will help, along with the NPQH programme, to bridge the gap that has often existed that requires new Heads to relearn all the skills themselves. The text is an attempt to enable the apprentice model of training Heads, as suggested by David Hargreaves, to be developed, so ensuring that skills are passed more quickly from one generation of Heads to the next in the same way that a new surgeon is trained by working with an experienced one.

chapter one

Introduction

0

What's in a name?

Leaders of schools have been called Head, Headteacher, Headmaster, Headmistress, Principal and Chief Executive. Schools have titles such as College and Academy as well. It is often bewildering to the outsider as to why there are so many names for what appears to be the same job. A clue can perhaps be found in the status of the two schools of which I have been the leader. The first began its life as a local comprehensive school although its public image was very much that of a specialist school. After two years that school became a grant-maintained Technology College and the legal status then reflected its public image. I am now 'Principal and Chief Executive' of a City Technology College. Its status is that of a private school funded by public money. The school is a registered company and has a board of trustees as well as a governing body. While schools remain schools then the title Head or Principal will survive. If they become Learning Networks and businesses then the title Chief Executive will become more appropriate.

Themes of the book

Every new job is a challenge and within the teaching profession, becoming a Head is the greatest challenge of all. You become the embodiment of the school and people will see you like that. Despite broader leadership teams and higher profile roles for governors you are still the figurehead.

In this first chapter the aim is to identify the themes involved in the job and thus in the book.

These are:

- the skills and differences between leadership, management and administration
- some of the preparation and development of the right attitude of mind required to do the job

- the importance of creating the right learning culture in today's schools and for tomorrow's adults

- succeeding chapters tackle details of how to develop some of the wide range of skills in leading and managing a school

- towards the end there is a short piece on managing the workload – a vital skill if you and your school are to flourish

- the final chapter looks to the future and what might be in store for schools

- throughout there is the assumption that you are intending to lead a school that seeks to improve constantly and that will aspire to become a 'world class school', since nothing less will do.

One of the best pieces of advice we have heard about successful school leaders is that they concentrate on the basics and do not try to take on too much. In the first year as a Head this is very important advice indeed.

Other very sound advice comes from the two professional associations for Heads, the Secondary Heads Association (SHA) and the National Association for Head Teachers (NAHT). Both have excellent booklets on what do on taking up a headship and we strongly advise that aspiring Heads and newly appointed Heads acquire one of them and tick off all the activities as they meet them. They also suggest things to avoid!

The professional associations also publish pamphlets on every aspect of the job from admissions to money to value added. But in our fast changing world we have to be more than just a person who pushes paper or manages paper. We have, as Drucker says, to become 'Change Leaders'.

The text tries to give a flavour of the different types of work and mental gymnastics that you have to go through every day. One of the first prerequisites is that you have to be physically fit and also mentally very tough. Continuing the gymnastics analogy, you have to be very fit in order to perform the routines without injury, and even fitter in order to make your actions look graceful, accomplished and stylish. It seems that the analogy holds true for headship.

So it would be fair to describe the book as a primer on headship. It is designed to help the reader understand the culture of the job, decide on priorities and to help define the discipline required for success. What it will not do is make you a good Head! No one ever learnt to ride a bicycle or drive a car by reading about it in a book. Again the analogy of the car driver is apt: only the driver can change direction, no one else. Much the same is true for schools: only you can make many of those decisions because it is you who holds the responsibility for the outcome of those decisions. The buck definitely stops at your door. This creates a whole new way of seeing the world.

Demands of a Head

Being the leader of a school or other educational organisation in an ever more rapidly changing world requires wanting to do the job, having the nerve to do the job and being prepared to make the mistakes that are an integral part of the learning process.

In the recent reassessment for Investors In People that occurred at a school, the inspector commented that he had never come across so many people that had this questioning approach to their work: 'We have done it this way now but we are always encouraged to ask "can we do it better next time?"' In essence that sums up the essential philosophy of the self improving school (or Total Quality Management which is explained in Chapter 2). This is very much a culture that is fundamental for schools in the future.

'Being a Head is a great job – especially if you don't weaken' is a statement that has been reported over many years. There is a great deal of sense in it. One of the first things to do as a Head is ensure that you have a good network of colleagues in whom you can confide and seek support. The bonds formed through these exchanges are deep and can be very rewarding. They also help to keep your feet on the ground. These links are very powerful mechanisms for support and relief when times get tough – as they most certainly will.

The pressures on a Head are enormous. Without considering any of the challenges, tasks and day-to-day issues that have to be dealt with, it is salutary to examine just how many people need to be able to have access to the Head in a school. This will then give you the idea of how many people think they have a right of access to you, and in an increasingly customer-led service we have to be available to all our customers, whoever they may be.

The numbers work out like this: in a school of 1000 students, there are likely to be about 100 staff consisting of teachers and support workers. Each student has at least two parents and although this may sound odd, if you interpret the Childrens Act, a child can have up to nine legal parents! It is therefore fair to say that even in these days of very mixed families, there are, on average, two adults to every child at your school. This immediately makes 3000 people who feel they have an immediate right of access to the Head. If you take each member of staff, they and their partners feel they have right of access to the Head, this adds another 200. If you then add all the governors, LEA officials, DfEE officers and all the significant members of the local community – which can easily come to another 300 people – you find that you have a number around 3500. If you give each of these people one hour of your time a year, you have a total of 3500 hours to give just in talking to them. If you work 70 hours a week, which is only just over the average for headteachers, then 50 weeks are required to give people the time that they would feel they deserve. But what about all those other tasks you have to do? Answering the mail, observing teachers teaching, preparing for and attending governors' and other meetings, appraisal interviews, job interviews ... The list goes on and on and you soon realise that the most you can offer other people of your time amounts to on average about ten minutes per person per year.

All right, it is fortunate that most parents do not wish to see you personally every year, nor do many of the local community expect that amount of time, but you have to remember that every time someone does wish to see you, you have to be fair to them and give them time to explain why they wish to see you, listen carefully to what they are saying and respond appropriately. They are due that attention, they do have to be valued and shown due respect by you. What this calculation does give you is a means of judging when someone is taking too much of your time unfairly. Learn to balance priorities – that is very much what the job is about at the top level.

Summary

Our intention is that, at the end of this chapter, you will have:

- acknowledged that the role and title of the Headteacher are changing
- owned that the responsibility for your decisions is yours alone – 'the buck stops here'.
- recognised that a large number of people want access to you and that good time management is essential.

chapter two

Leadership, management and administration

Introduction

The job of being a Head can be divided up into three parts: leadership, management and administration. Each of these three areas has a wealth of literature on it. This chapter aims to outline some of the specific aspects of each, particularly as they relate to headship now, and as they might in the near future. The three parts are interlinked and cannot be separated. At different times one aspect may have more relevance than another. In our current period of upheaval it is leadership which is mostly required, because at times of uncertainty we seek out people who can give us direction and purpose.

FIG. 2.1 The inter-relationship of leadership, management and administration

The essential focus of the job has become leadership. Twenty years ago you could be an excellent Head by just being an excellent manager and administrator. That is no longer the case. The reasons are linked to the changing relationship of the school to the outside world. Twenty years ago the leadership function was in the hands of the Local Education Authority (LEA) and Heads were expected to follow the policies laid down by the senior officers. Schools were places that had one specific function – to deliver education still very closely linked to the requirements of university entrance. There was little real accountability – it used to be said that you could never be too incompetent as a Head to be sacked! It was possible therefore, having been appointed as Head, to relax, mind the office, talk to the staff, entertain officials and governors and speak to the occasional parent and student. If the school didn't improve very much, well, that was fine, as long as it carried on doing the basic job and nobody was too challenged. You certainly weren't held accountable by today's standards. If there weren't too many disciplinary issues with students, well, that was fine too. There were still the issues of the day to be tackled, but they could be managed or administered to acceptable solutions. There was little drive to raise educational standards. At the time the pressures seemed intense to the postholders, but the bare facts of how many Heads sought early retirement then, as compared to now, speak for themselves.

Today, every aspect of the job of the Head is monitored from the moment you start. It may not be immediately obvious, but you always have to have one eye on the results next summer and one eye on the mail – in case that letter from Ofsted arrives. Even when setting up a new school the first public examination results will be published and scrutinised. This may be five years away but if you make a fundamental mistake that takes time to show, there will be no hiding place. The results are compared with the other local schools and your job will very soon be on the line if they do not come up to expectations.

That is how it should be, but most Heads have had little training to take on the running of a school to this level of public accountability or have the skills or experience of managing in such an environment. Nor have they had any training in managing the accountability or the publicity that goes with it. Fortunately this is being corrected with the National Professional Qualification for Headship (NPQH) becoming compulsory and the National College for School Leadership opening its doors soon.

There is a second logical consequence of this accountability: Heads must have the freedom to take the actions they think are appropriate. It is wrong and quite unacceptable for Heads and other teachers to be held responsible for the results of their students if they do not have the freedom (and responsibility) to take what they consider to be the most appropriate action at the particular moment. (Resources and finances willing.) As an example, there have been at least two Ofsted inspections of secondary schools where the schools have received reports that they had been put onto special measures because they had not achieved the required standard of education for their students. The reasons in both the reports was plain to see: the LEA, or the 'system', was at fault because it had not supported the school or its Head, despite years of requests for help. Yet in both cases it was the Heads who were in the dock and both had to resign. That was before Ofsted inspections of LEAs. More detailed reading of inspection reports on the Internet would almost certainly show further examples.

These are hard facts – no blame is being attached, it was as much the circumstances and the structures that existed as any individual's fault. Both at LEA level and school level, leadership was lacking, people knew there were problems but nobody was prepared to do enough, i.e. be bold enough and take responsibility for action, to make a difference. The question that should be asked is: had any one at the LEAs or in the schools had any relevant leadership training? It is not just asking for help or receiving the request for assistance that matters, it is the judgement that action needs to be taken, in the right way, at the right time and with the support of the necessary people. Most skills that existing Heads have acquired have been absorbed by working closely, as deputies, with good or outstanding Heads. As a profession we need to do better than this. The NPQH programmes and the Leadership Programme for Serving Heads (LPSH) programmes are a very good start. Any Head or aspiring Head should be taking part in one of these programmes or be about to do so.

So, what is leadership and how can you develop it or train it within you? How does it relate to management or administration?

Leadership

Leadership is about your vision of life, your principles and your determination to stand up for them. Leadership is being passionate about turning that vision into a reality. You have got to want to be in charge!

'It's a great life, if you don't weaken' is a phrase used by many successful people in different walks of life and by many successful Heads.

Whatever your vision or philosophy of life and education is, you have to develop it for yourself, you cannot take someone else's because *you* don't really believe it and you will quickly be shown up as a sham. Over a period of time you will have found certain views in life, certain philosophies/religions whose ideas you have come to espouse, want to follow and have faith in. You will have established a set of principles for yourself by which you try to live your life. So far this may have happened unconsciously.

TASK 1

Defining your principles

Reflect on your principles. Consider what really matters to you, then write down your own 'ten commandments' (or however many you have) by which you live your life. Then decide on whether these are values or principles. If they are values delete them and reflect further to make sure you identify your key *principles*.

This is an activity you need to practise regularly. It is of enormous benefit when you have really tough decisions to make and it is not easy to know what is the best 'next step'. Reflection back to your own principles invariably helps to make that decision clearer, easier to make, but not necessarily any easier to take.

You most certainly need to understand the difference between values and principles. *First things first* written by Stephen Covey with A. Roger Merrill, is an excellent text that gives guidance on how to find out what really matters to you and how to apply these principles in your life. (The better known text of Stephen Covey's is *The Seven Habits of Highly Effective People* and we strongly recommend that all aspiring and existing Heads read this. In it the author identifies seven essential ways of living that appear to be common to all successful people.)

Once you are certain of what matters then you can start applying it in your life and it is surprising how simple some decisions can become, providing you stick to your principles and don't weaken.

It is very important not to be deflected from your goal. Your vision is sacrosanct and every day you will find there are many pressures and siren voices that seek to deflect you from your purpose. You do have to be strong and you will have to upset some people, but overall, if you do not let anyone or anything deflect you, you will gain respect and, most importantly, be able to sleep at night. Both of these are crucial to your wellbeing. If either starts to give you cause for concern, act immediately and seek support from your personal network of professional contacts as well as from your friends and family. You cannot possibly continue for more than a very short period of time 'just hoping that things will get better'; they almost never do, but they frequently get worse.

Nonetheless, the practical reality is that you are human and you will make mistakes or forget to do something essential, from time to time. The trick (skill) is in having enough knowledge and sensitivity to read the signs, listen to them and to do something before the error or mistake is either noticed or before it becomes serious. If this requires the consumption of some humble pie and apologising for the error, then so be it. Admission of error shows your humanity and, providing it does not happen too often, will strengthen you personally and professionally.

There is a school of headship which says you should never admit your mistakes. If you subscribe to this view then you have to have a certain style of leadership, but you obviously cannot make too many mistakes or your competence will very quickly be questioned. However, if you are right all the time it is very easy to appear arrogant and acceptance of mistakes to re-establish that you are human can be a very invigorating process for all parts of the organisation.

In order to retain your sanity you do have to find and retain balance – this is achieved by having one or more activities which are wholly engrossing and which take you completely away from yourself. This needs to be done at least once a week for a few hours.

Leadership then is about being strong-minded and conveying your vision successfully to those around you. They must all believe in you and have faith in the vision. In the hugely readable and light-hearted book *The leadership secrets of Attila the Hun*, the author, Wess Roberts, uses the life of one of the most well known, but often despised, names in history to describe the many characteristics leaders need to have and to develop to be successful. He also uses the analogy to describe the sort of culture that a successful organisation should have.

Roberts outlines a range of qualities required of any strong leader. They are listed in Table 2.1 below with some paraphrasing and additions.

TABLE 2.1 The qualities of a strong leader

Loyalty	The ability to inspire this in your staff and not to tolerate disloyalty (not the same as disagreement).
Courage	Having the capacity to be fearless and strong! To be able to contend with periods of loneliness and rejection that all leaders have to face.
Desire	Having a strong personal desire to influence people, processes and outcomes
Emotional stamina	Each succeedingly higher level of leadership places increasing demands on your emotions. You need to have the capacity to recover quickly from disappointment without losing perspective as well as having the emotional strength to persist in the face of seemingly difficult circumstances.

Physical stamina   The demands of the job are physically tiring and physical fitness and good health are important.

Empathy   Leaders have to develop an appreciation for and an understanding of the values and culture of others. They have to use this to become good diplomats.

Decisiveness   Know the facts, weigh up the odds and take action. Don't vacillate or procrastinate. Remember it can be right to decide to do nothing now but the reasons for such decisions have to be clearly spelt out.

Anticipation   Learning by observation and through instincts sharpened by tested experience, leaders need to anticipate thoughts, actions and consequences. Anticipation bears a level of risk that is willingly accepted by the Head, who will excel when others turn to the comfort of personal security.

Timing   Essential to acts of leadership is the timing of actions and recommendations. There is no magic formula for developing this sense of timing. One often gains this leadership skill by lessons learned through failure.

Competitiveness   An intrinsic desire to win or be best is an essential quality of leadership. It is not necessary to win all the time, but it is necessary to win the important, principle/mission-related contests.

Self-confidence   Proper training and experience develop a personal feeling of assurance that is needed to meet the inherent challenges of leadership. Showing a lack of self-confidence is always interpreted as a sign of weakness and should never be given.

Accountability   Learning to account for personal actions and those of your staff is fundamental to leadership. This aspect of leadership is something that all staff in schools are increasingly having to master.

Responsibility   As leader, you are always responsible for your actions and for your school or organisation. As a Head you are also responsible in law.

Credibility   The words and actions of Heads have to be believable to all their many audiences. They must be trusted to

	have the intelligence and integrity to provide the correct information.
Tenacity	The quality of unyielding drive to accomplish assignments is an essential quality of leadership. Pertinacity is often the key to achieving difficult or challenging goals.
Dependability	If, as a Head, you cannot be depended on at all times to carry out your roles and responsibilities, then you shouldn't be seeking headship.
Stewardship	Heads and all leaders must serve in a manner that encourages confidence, trust and loyalty. Heads are caretakers of the education and wellbeing of the students and staff they serve and of the interests of the parents and the community they serve.
Humour	Don't take yourself too seriously otherwise you will quickly become enamoured and blinded by your own importance. Keeping a sense of fun about life, however tough it may sometimes get, helps maintain a sense of proportion.
Humility	As a steward you are in your job to serve others, never forget that.

These qualities of leadership take time to acquire and cannot be overly rushed. There are no short cuts to 'experience' and 'learning from failure' upon which so much of the job of leader depends, unless of course your name is Alexander of Macedon. Some will learn faster than others. These are simply rare opportunities to accelerate competence, and without paying the price, no matter how great or small, you cannot become properly prepared for leadership.

TASK 2

Analysing your leadership qualities

Read through the leadership qualities listed in Table 2.1 and then write down how much of each you think you have acquired. In a separate column, list the training and experiences from which that quality has developed. An example is shown below in Table 2.2.

TABLE 2.2 Leadership quality analysis

Competence	Training	Experience
Courage	(i) Completing army endurance course (ii) Completed London Marathon	(i) Refused to strike during industrial action in 1980s – vilified and isolated by other staff. (ii) Refused to be bullied by HoD in early career.
Tenacity	As above	Introduced new scheme of work as HoD which was disliked by staff. Took two years to be accepted, now standard practice and well liked by all.

When you have completed this part of the Task, score yourself on the level of your competence, using a grading system of 1= highest, 5= no competence.

With both parts complete, now discuss your self assessment with a close friend, mentor or partner. Ask them to judge you on the level of achievement they think you have reached. Discuss areas of disagreement. You will then need to plan some professional development.

———— Change leadership ————

Peter Drucker has written widely on management and leadership for over half a century and is one of the most widely respected professionals in this area. In his recent book *Management Challenges for the 21st Century*, he identifies tomorrow's key issues for businesses – both in the private and public sector, including schools and universities – and the strategies and principles involved in meeting the challenges. However, the role of the leader of the organisation, he suggests will become paramount as the pace of change continues to quicken. He suggests, that those organisations which will survive and flourish have to have 'change leaders' at the top. These are individuals who flourish on change – Drucker would describe them as 'thriving on chaos' – and who actively seek to *make* the future. Somewhat depressingly he suggests that many of those who do take this approach will fail, but he also says that all of those who do NOT try *will even more certainly fail*.

'One thing is certain for developed countries – and probably for the entire world: we face long years of profound changes. The changes are not primarily economic changes. They are not even primarily technological changes. They are changes in demography, in politics, in society, in philosophy and, above all, in world-view. ... It is futile to try to ignore the changes and to pretend that tomorrow will be like yesterday, only more so...

To try to make the future is highly risky. It is less risky, however, than not to try to make it.'

We as Heads have to become change leaders and the chapter on leadership later on concentrates on developing more of the skills of leadership of schools in today's world.

Management

The heart of the art of management is the capacity to get things done using whatever resources or lack of them that are available to you. To practise this art you have to acquire a set of skills and competences that can be identified, and have been by many people in a wide range of texts, but only learnt by experience. The significant difference between management and leadership relates to risk and vision. As deputy or head of department you can be an excellent manager by implementing the vision of the organisation using your skill to motivate people to find the right strategy to deliver a particular goal.

The literature on management is vast, but as the Head of a school that is aiming constantly to improve and to be among the best, because no other attitude is acceptable today, familiarity with the main texts of the major authors is essential. See *References* at the end of the book for some examples. The capacity to develop different management styles, ranging from the authoritarian to the democratic, is essential. Only from experience can you know when to use a particular one. When it is necessary to take 'command decisions' or 'executive decisions', it is important to tell those staff who might normally have expected to be involved in the decision-making process why you have not involved them in this particular case. You will need to retain their support.

There are also a number of management techniques that can be learnt. They can be applied in certain circumstances or become part of the culture of the organisation. In a school, which is a customer-focused, self-improving organisation, the basis of working should be quality and continuous improvement. These have developed from the principles of Total Quality Management and it is these standards that need to become the norm or endemic in the organisation.

Familiarity with Total Quality Management (TQM) and its techniques will pay great dividends since it contains many fundamental skills and processes that any competent manager needs to have. However, always be on your guard because not every part of TQM will suit you or your style. You have to develop that intuitive sense which knows what works for you and what does not.

The management style that you develop comes from, but is totally separate from, your leadership style. Leadership style can create buzz and motivation and a sense of purpose. Management style will create endemic cultural attitudes and teamworking skills. It will also get the best, or worst, from your staff and students. The leadership and management style you have will not be fixed but will vary depending on the state of the organisation you are in charge of and the nature of the relationships which exist within and between the staff.

Taken together, the two sets of skills and competencies that you have as the Head, define you – and thus your school – to the students and staff. The two together create a working culture that fits broadly into one of the four quadrants shown in Fig. 2.2 below. The target is to get as far into the lower right quadrant, quadrant 4, as possible.

FIG. 2.2 Stress/achievement quadrants

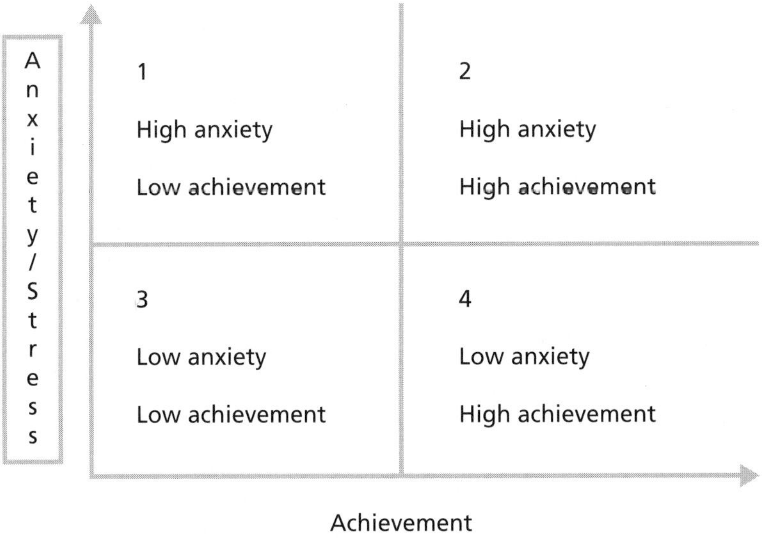

	1 High anxiety Low achievement	2 High anxiety High achievement
Anxiety / Stress	3 Low anxiety Low achievement	4 Low anxiety High achievement

Achievement

What does the organisation look like that fits into quadrant 4? Is your school there now and, if not, how are you going to take your organisation into it?

Table 2.3 shows some characteristics of schools in each quadrant.

TABLE 2.3 Stress/achievement quadrants – school characteristics

Quadrant 1 High anxiety/ low achievement	Quadrant 2 High anxiety/ high achievement	Quadrant 3 Low anxiety/ low achievement	Quadrant 4 Low anxiety/ high achievement
A failing school	'Satisfactory'	A coasting school	A very good school A 'Beacon' school
Stressed staff, not working together	Stressed staff, not working together	Staff drifting	Staff support each other, good teamworking
Senior staff blame others for failure; junior staff blame students and senior staff for failure	Poor link between departments and between junior staff and senior team	Staff feel well supported as are students; little attention paid to standards or accountability	All staff face up to responsibilities; there is a 'no blame' culture; strong self-improvement culture
Suspicious atmosphere, little trust	Individual working, little trust	Good support, often an open atmosphere and trust	Strong mutual support, open and trusting atmosphere
Poor leadership and management	Sometimes good leadership but poor management	Poor leadership but often satisfactory management	Strong leadership and very good management
Few rewards for staff and students, many sanctions	Rewards and sanctions often unfairly applied	Too many rewards for little achievements	Good balance of rewards and sanctions, usually fairy applied
Bullying likely to be common, but not recognised	Bullying likely to be common, known but tolerated	Little bullying publicly known about but may have undercurrents	Bullying rare, when it is known it is dealt with swiftly and satisfactorily

Quadrant 1 High anxiety/ low achievement	Quadrant 2 High anxiety/ high achievement	Quadrant 3 Low anxiety/ low achievement	Quadrant 4 Low anxiety/ high achievement
Students given little independence and responsibility	Students may be given independence and responsibility, but without accountability	Students have too much independence and responsibility with little accountability	Balance of independence, responsibility and accountability lead to ownership by students of the school's culture

These are just some of the features of the four kinds of culture that exist in organisations. It is unlikely that any organisation fits into one quadrant for all its activities, but while doing your job you want to move as many of them as possible into quadrant 4.

TASK 3

Analysing school activities

Using the characteristics described in Table 2.3 above, decide in which category you would place the following nine activities or parts of your school:

1 Senior management team

2 English Department

3 Science Department

4 Mathematics Department

5 The sixth form

6 The pastoral structure

7 Links with parents

8 Links with industry

9 Links with governors

While doing this exercise you will probably start to recognise specific differences between departments and areas of the school you are leading, studying or about to lead. This information will then help you to formulate the strategy you will need in order to bring each area into line with the school's vision and your planning.

———— Total Quality Management ————

For those unfamiliar with Total Quality Management (TQM) a summary of the process and principles is given next. TQM can be broken down into five stages shown in Table 2.4 below. It requires a range of quality improvement tools and also acts as a problem solving process. Each quality improvement tool fits into one of these stages and some tools can be used in more than one stage.

The stages are as follows and are sometimes known as the FADER process.

TABLE 2.4	The five stages of TQM
1 FOCUS	What is the problem?
	Make a clear statement of the problem to be solved.
2 ANALYSE	What is the cause of the problem?
	Collect data and evidence to identify the cause of the problem.
3 DEVELOP	Find a solution, preferably the best.
	Develop a solution that will permanently remove the cause of the problem.
4 EXECUTE	How to implement the solution?
	Develop and execute the action plan to implement the solution.
5 REVIEW	Did our solution have the desired effect?
	Measure the effect of the solution. The review may show the need for further analysis and development of more solutions.

The five stages to the Total Quality Management process form the basis of continuous improvement and the process when used properly is cyclical. The process is often described as a continuous improvement circle and every activity can be analysed and improved using the cycle. Figure 2.3 below illustrates this.

TQM is a process that always takes a view of an organisation from its customers' and clients' perspectives. The important first step is to define who your customers and clients are. In a school they are always the students and their parents, but for many parts of the school and its activities the customers and clients can be a wide range of other people and include staff as well. For example, the Learning Support Department, in addition to the parents and students whom they serve every day, also have all the heads of departments and all class teachers as their customers. The understanding that these teachers have of the Learning

Support Department, and their attitude towards it, are crucial to its success throughout the school.

FIG. 2.3 Continuous improvement circle

Thus TQM puts customers and clients at the heart of its process and allows them to define quality. The weakness of the process, from a Head's point of view, is that if you are not careful you can lose control of the agenda and the pace of development.

Quality improvement tools

The tools required for TQM are the normal range of activities that exist in any organisation, but they need to be used at the right time, in the right place and in the right way.

TABLE 2.5 Quality improvement tools

Tool	Use
Brainstorming	releases creativity, generates ideas
Nominal group technique	prioritises/values brainstorming ideas
Fishbone diagram	problem is put into 'the big picture', helps to find causes to problems and how they relate to each other

Tool	Use
Check sheet	for gathering evidence rather than opinion
Pareto analysis	bar chart for identifying the biggest problems and the main causes of problems
Force field analysis	display in 'T' shape of conflicting and restraining forces
Contingency diagram	turning the problem-solving process on its head. Brainstorm ideas to make the problem or cause worse or to prevent the solution from happening
Cost benefit analysis	finding best value between solutions
Action plans	checklist of what, when, how, who
Trend charts	using data in graphical form to monitor progress
Process flowchart	a chart that shows what happens in a process, who does what and the relationships between people in the process

The quality tools are used in different ways in different stages of the problem-solving process. Not every tool is used in every process. The matrix below indicates when the tools are most likely to be used in the different stages of the process.

TABLE 2.6 Quality tools matrix

	FOCUS	ANALYSE	DEVELOP	REVIEW
Brainstorming	*	*	*	*
Nominal group technique	*	*	*	*
Fishbone diagram		*		
Check sheet		*		
Pareto analysis		*		
Force field analysis			*	*
Contingency diagram	*		*	

	FOCUS	ANALYSE	DEVELOPE	EXECUTE	REVIEW
Cost benefit analysis			*	*	*
Action plans			*		
Trend chart				*	*
Process flowchart		*		*	

Any self-improving school will have taken aspects of the TQM process and integrated them into their normal school routines and procedures. Over time the procedures in use will have modified and it can pay dividends to go back to the fundamental process from time to time to ensure that current procedures are rigorous enough.

Management tells you what the customer wants and how well your organisation is doing at the moment. Leadership is knowing how far away you are from where you want to be, knowing what action you now need to take and, most importantly, taking it.

TASK 4

Applying TQM techniques

Take a problem that has recently been resolved and analyse the solution by applying a contingency diagram to it.

1 Draw an oval shape on a piece of paper as shown below. Inside write the problem. On the lines beside (you may want more than 5), write all the things you can think of that would make the problem worse! From this list you can generate a *prevention checklist*.

2 Now repeat the process, but put the solution you implemented in the oval and on the lines write all the things that will stop the solution from being properly implemented. Make sure that you have contingency plans ready to meet all the obstacles thrown up by the process.

FIG. 2.4 Prevention analysis skeleton

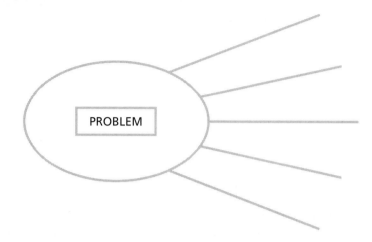

This task can be done by you on your own or it may be valuable if done as part of a senior team meeting.

New management systems are being developed all the time and this chapter is only designed to give a flavour. The above description of TQM is modified from that used by East Midlands Electricity. It is suggested that the latest techniques in use in your local business community will be worth exploring.

TASK 5

Contacting the local business community

Contact your local Chamber of Commerce and find which five local companies they regard as having some of the best management people and systems.

Find the name of one of the directors and arrange a visit of one hour's duration at each one.

Ask about their management and leadership practices and see if any could help you run your school better.

Offer them something in return, not necessarily straight away, but after the visit.

Before going make sure that you have ten questions about management issues that you want to talk about.

You will find some fascinating insights into the world of work, which will be enormously helpful to you, and others that will be less so. Increasingly you have a great deal to offer in return. You will find that management and training standards in many schools have many facets that are at least on a par and sometimes better than the best practice in business. Most importantly, of course, you have the next generation of employees for your local economy and a strong relationship with the key employers is a great benefit to both parties. As our knowledge society develops we in schools have knowledge management skills and techniques which command an increasingly high premium in the marketplace.

Working on your management skills and expertise is a constant activity for a Head today.

MBWA

Management By Walking About is a proactive management function which helps the leader or senior manager to keep his or her finger on the pulse. However, the practice has to be used properly to deliver the very powerful benefits claimed for the technique. The process involves forsaking the office for considerable periods of time and walking around the school asking everyone you meet questions which raise their sense of self worth and which give opinions and views about the impact of the decisions that the Head makes at the point of impact of those decisions. It is important to know what questions to ask, what praise needs to be given and, most importantly of all, how to interpret the responses. If these are achieved then MBWA is one of the most powerful of all leadership and management techniques.

TASK 6

Asking staff MBWA questions

Write down three questions that you would ask and what sort of responses you might expect when making a tour of the school and talking to staff, if:

- the results in the summer are much lower than everyone expected

- the results in the summer are much better than all the predictions

- you have just heard that a full Ofsted inspection is to take place in six weeks.

TASK 7

Asking students MBWA questions

Write down three questions that you might ask students to find out about their work when you sit down to have lunch with them. Repeat the exercise two or three times a week. What sort of responses will you expect? What will you do with the information? The responses will be given in language that comes from their view of life and from their agenda. The kinds of response that you receive comes in a number of forms:

- General information, which is based on personal experience. This helps to build a picture of the individual within the larger canvas of the school.

- Bright ideas that you want to implement, sometimes immediately.

- Information that links together.

As a general rule, if three pieces of information gained from different sources are closely linked, then it will be prudent to take immediate action – either positive or negative. For example, if you have a new teacher in the school and students from three different years comment on how much they are enjoying the subject with this teacher, then a word or two of praise in the appropriate manner to the teacher would be sensible. This information might have been gathered by asking 'What is your favourite subject this year?' Followed by 'Why that one?' In similar fashion the opposite question can be asked 'Which is your least favourite subject at the moment?' Followed by 'Why do you think that is?' Three negative answers about the same teacher require a response which might be a discussion with the head of department or subject leader to monitor the work of that member of staff and offer additional support to him or her.

Unless you are out of school altogether, it is strongly recommended that some MBWA should happen everyday. Whenever possible seek to encourage and praise staff and students for their efforts.

A version of MBWA was carried out for many years by a Head in the South West of England who would suddenly stop discussions and say to the person he was with: 'Let's go and find someone to say "Well done and thank you to". I am sure it won't be difficult.' Staff and students thus looked forward to meeting the Head on these tours and all felt much more valued after his visits. However, he was also well known for not tolerating shoddy work! *Expectations were high and people were valued.*

Administration

The third area of the job of a Head is the least glamorous, but the one that can have the most positive effect on morale and attitudes within your organisation. Being a good administrator is not quite such a prerequisite to being a good Head as are management skills and leadership ability. Nonetheless the capacity to know what good administration is and the ability to ensure that the right staff and systems are in place are essential. The Head then needs to have had significant experience in dealing with the administrative functions within an organisation before taking up a post. If you have been a head of a department then you will have already spent many hours on administrative tasks since it is most unlikely that you will have had significant support from office staff in that role.

Administration is about logistics. It is the management of things rather than people. Making sure that everyone gets enough food at the right time every day and that everyone gets to the right classroom at the proper time with the relevant teacher are all vital administrative functions that have to be correct for the smooth running of the organisation. Too often teachers and senior staff, including the Head, appear to underestimate the value of the administrative and support staff of the school, and too many schools use teachers as very expensive administrators. This is easily done simply because we do not spend enough time listening to the support staff and hence valuing them properly. Do you consult the support staff when considering a change to the reward system for students? The view of the support staff will be very informative and gives a completely different picture from that of the teaching staff. If they have to administer the system then they should be consulted about change. They will also have a different perspective on how the change will affect the students as their relationship with the students will be different from the teachers'. If your organisation is an Investor In People then the above will already be familiar.

Administration is about the practical ways of turning leadership and management plans into reality. It is not usually so exciting but certainly no less important than the other two aspects. What Heads have to take great care over is that they do not hide behind administrative tasks when they should be out there leading and managing. We all do this from time to time as there is less emotional stress in administration and sometimes we need to draw back from the daily mental challenge of leading and managing. There is nothing wrong with this, as becoming engrossed in an administrative task can be not only therapeutic but also gives you a deeper insight into the way your organisation functions. In turn you then gain the knowledge you need to take decisions in other areas. However, I repeat, do not let yourself become submerged in administrative tasks for too long as you will not be leading or managing as effectively as you need to.

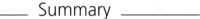

Summary

Our intention is that, at the end of this chapter, you will have:

- seen that Headship comprises three main types of work: leadership, management and administration
- recognised that leadership is crucial to the success of a school, especially in our rapidly changing world today
- identified your principles and values – critical in successful leadership
- analysed your leadership skills and their source
- applied a TQM tool to a problem you have faced
- devised questions to use when practising the technique of Management by Walking About (MBWA)
- considered the function of administration and the role of administrators in maintaining momentum and morale in the organisation.

chapter three

Preparing for headship

Introduction

The job of being a Head has never been more challenging but at the same time has never been more rewarding than it is today. It has changed beyond recognition and will change still further in the next few years. How do you prepare for such a role? The capacity for constant change and a love of complexity and crisis are all essential ingredients in the skills basket of the aspiring Headteacher, Principal or Chief Executive of a 'school'.

TASK 8

Personal assessment

Before embarking on any official training programme it will pay dividends to ask a number of questions.

1 Why do I want to be a Head/Principal/Chief Executive?

2 Am I aware of the impact on my life and those around me if I become a Head?

3 How will I cope with the additional public profile? (Usually only local, but increasingly the chance of national publicity seems to come with the job.)

4 Is my cup always half-full or half-empty?

5 Can I 'meet with Triumph and Disaster and treat those two impostors just the same'?

It is unlikely that clear answers can be given at any time to these questions, but they will have to be faced. Discussing them with friends and family before starting out on the preparation will certainly help you to be better able to find answers that can be understood by others. Many of the decisions that you have to take as a Head require a toughness that can be quite debilitating and which can put a lot of pressure on your personal and professional relationships. Coming to terms with the impact of this decision making with your family and friends will have significant consequences for you and them.

Can you look someone in the eye and say, 'Based on the evidence collected, you are an incompetent teacher and I'm dismissing you,' and live with it?

_____ Role of the Head _____

The NPQH programme is becoming mandatory for new Heads and outlines the skills and knowledge which have to be acquired and proven to be up to the right standard before anyone can become a Head. Initially the programme defines the core purpose of the Head as:

> 'The leading professional in the school. Working with the governing body, the Headteacher provides vision, leadership and direction for the school and ensures that it is managed and organised to meet its aims and targets.'

It continues with a list of other core tasks:

> Continuous improvement in the quality of education
>
> Raising standards
>
> Ensuring equality of opportunity
>
> Development of policies and practices
>
> Resources are efficiently and effectively deployed to meet aims and objectives
>
> Secure the commitment of the wider community of the school
>
> Develop effective networks with all the right people and organisations.

Not to mention:

> Being responsible for creating and maintaining a productive, disciplined learning environment and for the day to day management, organisation and administration of the school.

It is interesting to note that the most important and fundamental task from which all others flow is listed last. We cannot create world class schools, world class learning networks or world class learning communities unless we first create and maintain productive disciplined learning environments in any organisational framework. We cannot maintain schools as we have known them but in preparing to make the changes necessary for the future we have to make certain that we do not abandon the fundamentals. The basic rules of life have always been there and always will be. In different ages we find different words to describe them, but they are personal self discipline, dignity and respect for others. All human societies have these in some form or other and the capacity to instil these in everyone is the first and most important task of the Head. It is from these that motivation, commitment, expectation and loyalty flow.

In addition to the above list should also be added:

- the role of Chief Executive
- the need for business acumen
- skills in entrepreneurship
- the need to develop world wide networks

and always a: *'Passion for Excellence'*.

Business leadership

In preparing for Headship the desire to make the school that you lead anything other than outstanding is no longer good enough. The Head is also becoming the leader of a business that is expanding and becoming reliant on the organisation's capacity to make money as well as to spend it efficiently and effectively. This has happened to the university and further education sector and there is no reason to suppose that it will not happen to the school sector. It has been going on for years in many small ways in schools but we have to change from taking an amateurish view to a professional approach. The independent sector has always had such an approach, the State sector can no longer pretend otherwise. If the government cannot provide a funding level to match the independent sector then State schools have to find ways to achieve it themselves. So part of the preparation for Headship must now include some business management training.

Change leadership

Drucker in his book *Management Challenges for the 21st Century* is very certain that the only successful leaders in the next few decades will be those who can manage and, more importantly, *lead* change. He talks about developing a capacity to 'make the future' and that such leaders are called 'change leaders'.

This requires always being optimistic, often against what seem overwhelming odds, and always trying to find a better way to do things. These must go hand in hand with high expectations. In fact this approach is now an essential ingredient in the repertoire of skills needed to be a Head.

Being a change leader means becoming a risk taker, i.e. gaining the entrepreneurial skills and the confidence to use them. This will have frightened many existing and potential Heads immediately, because they will say, 'We must not take risks with our children's education because we are here to care for and to look after their interests and it is inappropriate to experiment with their education.' Drucker's, and many other thinkers', point of view now is that far greater risks are taken by *not* doing anything and trying to maintain the status quo for children's education than are involved in implementing the changes that will properly prepare our young people for the world of tomorrow.

So, how do you gain this mindset?

First, the most important skill you need is the right frame of mind. Anything less and you will fail. The American approach – 'Ya just dooo it!' has a great deal to commend it, and as soon as you have convinced yourself and your senior team that the change you wish to implement is right, then this can be and should be the right approach. Notwithstanding, of course, the need to take everyone with you and all the other caveats... This requires everyone in the organisation also to acquire the appropriate frame of mind, otherwise it is very easy for the Jeremiahs to put the brake on development.

You now also need to gain an understanding of how people think, react and make decisions.

Emotional intelligence

An ability to understand and make use of emotional intelligence as described by Goleman in his books *Emotional Intelligence* and *Working with Emotional Intelligence*, is increasingly important.

Emotional intelligence is that capacity to respond through your feelings to events. The ability to manage and develop emotional intelligence in others is an important part of every teacher's role. Most do it unconsciously every day. As a Head there is a need to have a greater understanding of the role of emotional intelligence in life and the value and importance of understanding it as a leader. All great leaders know how, under certain conditions, they can manipulate the emotions of their followers. Hitler and Stalin managed it very well with disastrous consequences for all their people. Churchill and Roosevelt managed it well enough to lead their peoples to success against tyranny. It seems from personal observation that the power to affect the emotions of young people in the appropriate manner is one of the key ingredients in successful headship.

Some people seem to have this capacity from the way they work and behave as if it was a natural talent. Perhaps it is. Others of us have to work at gaining the necessary perception and using a reference source and a mentor can build this capacity considerably. Leadership itself certainly involves the capacity to manage one's own emotional intelligence as well as that of others.

TASK 9

Understanding emotional intelligence

If you have not already done so, read Goleman's books, *Emotional Intelligence* and *Working with Emotional Intelligence*.

In *Emotional Intelligence*, Goleman lists eight families of emotions:

- Anger — fury, outrage, and so on.

- Sadness — grief, gloom, despair …

- Fear — anxiety, concern, terror …

- Enjoyment — happiness, joy, ecstasy …

- Love — friendliness, trust, agape …

- Surprise — shock, wonder, amazement …

- Disgust — contempt, scorn, revulsion

- Shame — guilt, embarrassment, remorse, contrition …

Take each of these families and list three other emotions within each.

Where might you put jealousy?

What of virtues such as faith, hope, courage?

What of vices such as doubt, complacency and sloth?

Goleman suggests these questions and does not have ready answers. However, the need to better understand our emotions seems most important. As Aristotle put it:

> Anyone can become angry – that is easy. But to be angry with the right person, to the right degree, at the right time, for the right purpose, and in the right way – that is not easy.' (The Nicomachean Ethics)

Multiple intelligences

Howard Gardner has written widely on the nature of academic intelligence and his work has been developed by others. It is now generally accepted that there are many, or multiple, intelligences which we each have in different proportions. Those normally listed are:

- linguistic/verbal
- mathematical/logical
- spatial/visual
- kinesthetic/body
- intrapersonal
- interpersonal
- scientific
- musical/rhythmic
- environmental.

TASK 10

Understanding multiple intelligences

If you are not already familiar with them, read some of Gardner's work, for example: *Frames of Mind*, *The Unschooled Mind* and *Leading Minds*.

The implications, we know, have already started to have a profound impact on learning. Gardner puts it this way:

> 'It's my belief that virtually any topic and concept can be approached in a number of ways, and that optimal teaching makes it possible for the largest range of students to learn about the range of human knowledge. ... Teachers should be able to present materials using several intelligences; and learners – intrapersonally intelligent about themselves should be able to bootstrap themselves to superior understanding in a way most appropriate to their own cognitive profile.'

—————— Changing the culture ——————

Next you need to learn how to create a culture that is not afraid of failure and that removes the blame culture from your school and staff room. Schools are organisations that have been paternalistic, the Head after all is *in loco parentis*, and education has been a risk averse business. Schools have thus become too safe academically, but life is a risky business and proper preparation for it must allow more risk in learning – and especially creativity – than we have previously tolerated. The staff room is an important place to start because it is always the attitude of staff which is so important when implementing change. If they do not feel confident about taking risks, i.e. they will be blamed if an new idea does not work as expected, they won't take them.

—————— Embrace technology ——————

There is only one chapter in the book on technology, but in preparation for becoming a Head it is very important to gain as much understanding and liking for new technology and its impact on society as possible. However weak your background we think it is vital to have as deep a knowledge as possible of the technological process because so much decision making in our society is based on it. Second, unless we are aware of the power and pace of change that technology is releasing, it is difficult to manage – and even more difficult to lead – the change processes in our modern world.

TASK 11

Developing a future view

Read *The Road Ahead* by Bill Gates and also the more recent *Business @ the Speed of Thought*. Here are some quotes about the book by Gates from the comments on the Amazon.com web site:

> '"Business is going to change more in the next ten years than it has in the last fifty," Gates states in the book's introduction.'
>
> '"I wrote *Business @ the Speed of Thought* because technology is changing everything," Gates said. "I wanted to give business people and other organisational leaders a road map that shows how they can take advantage of the incredible opportunities of the digital age."

At the heart of the new economy, Gates says, is a new way of doing business, using fast, accurate information to plan the right product, deliver unparalleled customer service, empower workers and react to changes in the marketplace. "How you use information will determine whether your business thrives or fails," he says.'

'"The successful companies of the next decade," Gates writes, "will be the ones that use digital tools to reinvent the way they work." A central theme is the empowerment of people, from lower-level employees who can use information to lift the nature and quality of their work, to the CEO, who can use better information to drive the company's strategic direction. Gates outlines twelve steps that business should take to make certain they're getting the most out of their technology investments to get smarter workers, more effective overall corporate performance, and more satisfied customers.

1. Integrate e-mail into your organization so that you can act on news with reflex-like speed.

2. Use digital tools to get information out to everyone, to analyze important business data, and to share insights.

3. Automate routine tasks so workers are free to think.

4. Use technology to create virtual teams.

5. Replace paper forms with efficient on-line forms.

6. Use digital tools to replace one-task jobs with jobs that add value.

7. Use digital tools to get feedback on products fast, and use the feedback to improve quality faster.

8. Use technology to redefine your business and expand your boundaries.

9. Use technology to deliver new kinds of customer service.

10. Trade information for time, becoming a just-in-time operation.

11. Eliminate the middleman and deal directly with customers. If you are a middleman, use the technology to add value.

12. Let customers solve their own problems using new technology.

"The typical company has made 80 percent of the investment in the technology that can give it a healthy flow of information, yet is typically getting only 20 percent of the benefits that are now possible," Gates notes. Success, Gates says, requires a company to build a digital nervous system,

> which he describes as the organizational equivalent of the human nervous system, "providing a well-integrated flow of information to the right part of the organization at the right time."'

For 'business' read 'education', for if anyone doubts that education is not now a business we think they are deluding themselves. The very title 'Knowledge Society' shouts this fact in our faces. It is likely, however, that the nature of business will change somewhat and we as educators have to lead this transformation in collaboration and partnership with society's other leaders.

Triangulation

Experience suggests that things happen in threes. The old saying that 'Bad things happen in threes' seems to be borne out in practice. The 'rule of three' can be a very powerful tool for leaders in their daily lives. The principle is very simple: if the same person, issue, problem arises three times in a short space of time, action needs to be taken. What that action is will depend on the situation, but normally it makes sense to gather more information about the person or situation. Then use the data to find the cause of the problem and then take action. Invariably if the signs are ignored the situation will get worse and it will be much more difficult to resolve later.

The principle of three also works in many other situations. Ofsted frequently use it for gathering evidence – written policy, known by staff, in action with students – on which judgements are based.

Decision making

As a Head the number of decisions that have to be taken every day about so many different things can be very large indeed. Frequently others will try to rush you into an action – 'We need to act immediately on this'. However, it is quite often appropriate not to be rushed into a decision because an individual tries to pressure you into it. It can be an active decision to consider deliberately an issue and decide that this is not the time or the moment to make a decision. The old saying 'Act in haste and repent at leisure' is never more true than when you are a Head. It is essential though to make sure you are not sweeping an issue under the carpet. Make a note of the issue and put it in your 'hold' folder that you look at, about once a week, until you 'know' it is time to decide. 'Knowing' in this sense only comes from experience and practice, frequently gained from hindsight when reflecting back on why something worked out wrongly. Examine why it went wrong and then see if it is possible to identify a moment when action should have been taken. Make a note of it and remember it for the future.

Delegation

There are so many things to monitor each day that you increasingly 'do' less and less of a day-to-day nature. There is a need to ensure that your senior team have the space to, can, and do, take control of day-to-day matters. You have to have trust in them and they in you. Trust will be there initially because of your position. As Head you have to show your confidence in your senior team by giving them individually opportunities to deliver projects and activities without your intervention. However, you must maintain your monitoring role.

If you do interfere then staff will be reluctant to take on the task or responsibility for it and you will end up with an unbearable burden to carry personally. Too much abnegation, on the other hand, will lead to tasks either not being done or being done badly and then you will have to take on your superman role again to get things right. As with most things in life, balance counts and the skill is in reading the signs that tell you your school or that activity is in balance. How do you do this?

For any activity decide what you think is important and what are the key signs of successful development – performance indicators, if you want the jargon.

Then make notes on future dates in your diary to check the progress of the activity against your indicators. When the time comes, check them and take action only if you need to. If things are going well remember to praise and encourage.

CASE STUDY

Monitoring activity

Two activities taken from a secondary school help to indicate what sort of monitoring is required of activities in a school.

Activity 1 – Work Experience

Each year in July Year 10 and Year 12 students have two weeks' work experience. The Head of Careers, who coordinates work experience, visits the Head in the first month (September) of the Head's tenure and explains his role and how the work experience programme operates. He leaves the Head with a diary of events for careers and work experience.

One month later the Head notices that there is a wide range of job advertisements on the careers noticeboard and that there is a note for all Y10 tutors in the weekly bulletin about work experience. In the meantime there are regular requests by the Head of Careers and his deputy to have Tuesday afternoon out of school to make health and safety visits to a range of local employers.

In February the Head is asked to approve the letter that goes out to all parents of Y10 students, individually addressed with details of the placements and the programme. The Head is invited to address the parents' meeting in June to go over final arrangements.

Activity 2 – Annual visit to Paris

The Modern Languages Department organises an annual visit to Paris. This year the visit is to take place in February and the Head of Department has a meeting with the Head in September. The Head receives an outline of the programme. She sees the letter to parents inviting the post-16 students to take part which is sent out in early October. Nothing more is heard in the Head's office about the trip.

At Christmas the Head asks the Head of Department how progress is going. She is assured that all is in hand and that the Head of Department is monitoring the member of staff who is organising the visit. The Head is reassured, because the Head of Department has been organising and leading the annual school ski trip for the past three years and is very experienced in this area.

After Christmas the Head is very busy with admissions for next year and forgets to check with the trip organiser. Four days before the trip is due to depart the organiser rushes into the Head asking to have a letter approved to go out to the parents. The Head asks the organiser to go through all the things that still have to be done. The list is rather long. She calls in the Head of Department, who is embarrassed to have been let down but clearly knows that he has not been doing enough monitoring. The Head immediately cancels the trip and admonishes the Head of Department. She has a quiet word only with the young organiser and explains that if the organisation is not good enough at the preparation stage, then the risks when staff and students are under pressure overseas are too great. She is not prepared to let a young member of staff risk ruining his career.

—————— Summary ——————

Our intention is that, at the end of this chapter, you will have:

- assessed how headship is likely to affect your personal life
- recognised that a positive attitude and a passion for excellence are prerequisites for headship today
- developed an understanding of emotional intelligence and its importance
- familiarised yourself with Garcher's work on multiple intelligences and how it applies to an educational environment
- seen that it is increasingly important both for students to understand that there are multiple intelligences and for them to recognise which they are most proficient in so that they can maximise their learning opportunities
- recognised that the role of technology in society, and the direction it is taking us, are part of the essential raft of skills for a Head
- applied the 'rule of three' when taking action
- seen that making non-decisions can be as important as making active decisions
- developed the skill of delegation and know it is a fundamental tool for successful Heads.

chapter four

Creating a learning culture

Introduction

In the past, and even today, there exists in the consciousness of many people a mythical perception that teachers actually teach children. Observations over many years in the classroom make it painfully clear that this almost never happens. What we call teaching is, in fact, the teacher opening the mind of the student to want to receive information, the desire to gain understanding and the willingness to go through the pain of learning. All the actual learning takes place when the teacher is no longer trying to teach the student.

All right, there is some exaggeration here, but the parody is not far from the truth. What we have managed to do more successfully in recent years is to analyse how knowledge and skills are transmitted.

Students have access to information today in a way which has never been possible before. The Internet really does have the capacity to liberate the mind – to change the way we think, learn, work and live. Teaching is becoming the capacity to motivate students to want to learn and teaching them the skills of how to learn. They then go away from us and get on with the learning. We, the teachers, get in the way of learning if we are not very careful. What we have to do is create and maintain the context for the learning to happen. The context is the facts and figures of knowledge set out in a structure. Only when this has been done sufficiently strongly is it possible to start teaching children and students how to learn. To use a scientific analogy: the beauty of the human form is the outer shape, but this cannot exist unless the structure, the skeleton, is strong and developed enough to support the flesh and skin of the body.

TASK 12

Lesson observation

The next time you observe a lesson, record the times spent on the following activities:

1 The amount of time in the lesson when the teacher is actually teaching the class.

2 The amount of time the class spend being told facts and information by the teacher.

3 The amount of time the class spend finding out facts and information for themselves.

4 The amount of time the class spend on analysing and reflecting on the facts and information.

5 The amount of time the class spend, during the lesson, on applying the knowledge they have acquired.

Having done this exercise once, observe classes on a basis of one a week for the next year and record these facts. From the observations – which should also be carried out by other members of the senior team – build up a picture of how learning happens in the school you are working in or of which you are Head.

_____ Sanctions _____

Creating a culture that is naturally predisposed towards learning is not what schools have achieved in the past. In fact, although this has been the declared aim of school, the reality has frequently been the exact opposite. For example, take the simple case of punishments applied to students who have misbehaved in class, truanted or whatever. In the vast majority of cases the standard punishment will involve, amongst other things, a detention. During the detention the student will almost certainly be expected to do some written or other school work.

So what. SO WHAT!!

Most of us find it very hard to see the contradiction here. But what sense is there in saying on one day how much we want people to be lifelong learners and how much fun learning is, when on the next day, we are saying that learning is a punishment? We imply in giving learning work as a punishment that we think work is unpleasant and must be endured before you can go out and have fun which is in direct contradiction to what we are trying to achieve. No wonder the street-wise youngsters reject education when it is so contradictory and the teachers can't even see it!

TASK 13

Rewards and sanctions

Examine the rewards and sanctions that are applied in your school. Look at the impact and real meaning behind them.

Get a group of staff to work on them, look for contradictions and then produce a policy and procedure that are consistent with each other and the vision of the school.

Abandonment

Creating a learning culture requires this search for consistency and the eradication of contradiction in the habits and practices that have grown up in schools. One simple example of eradication or, as Brain Caldwell calls it, abandonment, that radically alters culture is the switching off of the bell as the manager of our daily routines in school. It does not lead to chaos and anarchy but to a more civilised, quieter, and more purposeful learning environment. How can this be? Let us look at the reasons for having a bell in the first place.

Originally in schools, as elsewhere in life, there were few clocks. Life revolved around the chime of the church clock if anyone needed to know the time. During the industrial revolution, many people moved to the cities and into factories. These factories introduced sirens to summon the workforce in the morning and to tell people when breaks, lunch and the end of the working day were.

When schools started for everyone, the lessons could only be identified by hand bells that were rung to summon the children into the school. As the school day became more complex, the bell was rung for the change in activities. When electricity was brought into the school the lesson changes could be automated by having a bell linked to the electricity supply and clock. This became ever more complex during the 20th century.

Clocks then started appearing in all classrooms and teachers and students started acquiring timepieces of their own. Soon they became digital and it was possible for every student to know the time to one hundredth of a second. Still lessons in most secondary schools were managed by a bell. In fact, because everyone could tell the time so accurately, it became something of a sport to point out that the school clock was no longer accurate and that yesterday it had been out by as much as 2.157 seconds!

Meanwhile, in the rest of society, organisations and the world of work moved on. How many other activities in our society are today regulated by bells? Everyone, including our children from the age of five, can tell the time. As soon as we allow children out of our sight, we ask them to be back home by a certain time. They know they have to be and we, their parents, get worried very quickly if they do not turn up. Now we even go so far as to make sure they have their own mobile phones so that they can contact us to make sure we don't worry too much about them. On the front of each mobile phone is a digital clock!

So why on earth do we need to ring bells for the beginning and end of lessons any more? Are not students and teachers capable enough to be responsible for their own teaching and learning within the school when they are quite capable of running their own lives as soon as they walk out the front gates?

We think it is demeaning to all of our community to have to treat them like some latter day version of a Pavlovian experiment.

When the bells are switched off it is everyone's responsibility to be at the lesson at the right time. It is the teacher's responsibility to start and finish the lesson at the right time. If students are late for lessons then that is an issue for discussion, reprimand and punishment if needed.

What are the benefits? First the lesson starts at the published time. Students will move to the lesson to be there at, say, 11.00 for the start. If the bell goes for lessons to start at 11.00, nobody moves until the bell rings and then the lesson starts five minutes late. Second because lessons begin and end at the teacher's discretion, there is generally a three minute period during which lessons end. This leads to a staggered exit from classrooms. When this happens with 10 classes coming out of 10 classrooms on the same narrow corridor, it dramatically reduces congestion, which reduces tension and aggression. This leads to a calmer and quieter atmosphere around the school. Most importantly of all, staff and students gain ownership of time which makes them feel more in control and better valued. Consequently students are better motivated and thus become better learners.

TASK 14

Abandonment

What other fundamental practice in your school could, or perhaps should, be abandoned? Consider, for example, school reports. What is of value in them? Could they be replaced by a better system that properly reflects the way the rest of our society works?

Work out the consequences of not doing something that has been done for years and decide whether it is worth the risk of implementing the change. Pick your own example to work on next.

————— The modular culture —————

Just as learning how to learn requires structure, so too does creating a culture. The structures here are the framework and process that enable the culture to exist. These are such things as the type of day, the discipline and rewards structure, the uniform, the fixed points in the year, the learning cycle, the reporting structure. Given that a framework is needed, there is one that has been shown to be the cornerstone of school improvement – and making better schools is why we want to be Heads, isn't it? – and that is *the modular culture*. In the *Seven Habits of Highly Successful Schools* and in a recent study in Australia of most improved schools, there was one common feature in all of these and that was the modular approach to teaching, to learning and to life, although it may not have that title in all the schools.

The basis of the approach, which has been called the modular curriculum and modular learning, but now seems to encompass a way of life, includes a set of basics that need to be understood and lived to create the culture. The key features are:

- a fixed time for each unit of learning
- regular assessments and reporting
- learning goals known in advance
- learning methods discussed and agreed with students
- review and reflective time built in to the teaching day to consider progress and set new learning targets
- rewards and sanctions built in.

The intention of the process is to enhance the ownership of the learning process by the student. If lifelong learning is to mean anything it must ensure that by the time they leave school all young adults have a love of learning and a desire to continue studying. If that sounds a bit far fetched then it is only an ideal. In many instances we have a scenario where at 16, 80 per cent of students despise, or at best tolerate, learning and 20 per cent have a passion for it. We need to reverse these percentages. The modular culture is successful because:

- it puts the student at the centre of the learning process
- gives the student ownership of learning

- gives the teacher ownership of teaching
- raises expectations
- increases the self esteem of students.

CASE STUDY

Guidelines from a school for the implementation of modular learning and creating a culture that respects the needs of students first.

Learning Culture: Teaching Methods

General

1 Throughout the school we will teach by encouragement. It is our intention to create a natural learning culture throughout the school. It is a clearly defined method in this school that all teachers will endeavour to encourage students to believe in themselves. It is our belief that students will make much greater progress if they have defined tasks and targets, which are achievable. Above all else, students need to achieve success, and progress needs to be measured and benefit needs to be perceived by students as they work through relatively short-term tasks. Staff should spend a considerable amount of time in identifying learning needs, in identifying the correct pace at which students need to be taught. We should be very much aware that students need to have their dignity respected and they need to be taught at a pace with which they can cope.

2 The other crucial aspect required to create a learning culture is that students take responsibility for their own learning. To encourage this sense of responsibility there are no bells and all are expected to be able to manage their time properly and arrive for lessons promptly.

3 The school works in departments, each of which has a syllabus, a staff handbook and a resource bank. Each department works with and consults closely with all teachers to establish meaningful schemes of work based on the National Curriculum and our modular framework. Each scheme clearly defines skills, concepts, experiences and values. It identifies the varied teaching methods with which each topic can be taught. There is a set time limit for each topic and each topic will be evaluated. Students at all levels are encouraged to identify why a topic is being taught, what skills are being learned and to share in the evaluation and target-setting process. The usual time for each module is six weeks.

4 Students will be grouped in the most appropriate arrangements to maximise their learning. Consequently, in Year 7 we use mixed ability groups on entry for diagnostic purposes. Later on we use setting and banding to enable students to be effectively stretched. Children should be neither bored with work that is too easy, nor humiliated by work that is too difficult. There is a need for constant review to ensure teaching is rigorous and stimulating. It is important that the latest methods that are available and appropriate are used. This is where the development of resource banks is essential.

5 Resource banks should contain a list of both the teaching methods and materials which experience has indicated are the most useful and stimulating. There should be at least one resource bank for each year group. In most departments it will contain the following:

(i)   Network applications and software suitable for all levels of ability

(ii)   Internet and intranet sites of particular value

(iii)   CD ROMs, videos, TV programmes and films

(iv)   Projector slides and transparencies

(v)   Work sheets

(vi)   Cross reference to libraries and databases

(vii) Programmes for visits and homeworks

(viii) Curricular links and applications to the world of work

(ix)   In specialist subjects there will, of course, be a list of the available materials and equipment in, for example laboratories, workshops, libraries, and gymnasia. It is vital that departments should work cohesively with each other so that individual students can share skills, concepts and experiences in a meaningful way.

6 Able students will be stretched by stimulating and interesting work provided by all departments.

7 Students in need of special learning or adjustment will be withdrawn for short-stay support, guidance and help. It is not the policy of the school to use segregation whilst helping. It is our objective to ensure that all our students are stimulated and involved in all work in the learning environment.

8 We ensure that there is an interface between students and teachers on a regular basis. We are very concerned that note taking and copying should only rarely be used as part of our work. In the last analysis we will work constantly to ensure that methods are used that will encourage students to ask questions regularly, to share in the learning process, to discuss their work and to acquire their education in an atmosphere of mutual respect, encouragement and interest.

9 The school has a clear homework policy that is regularly reviewed. Basically, we believe it is important that young people should continue with their research, revision and learning on a regular basis.

Wherever possible this homework should be stimulating and challenging. It should be based on the plans to involve young people in the process of learning and the process of identifying clear tasks that will help them to achieve success.

10 We will encourage students to be involved in problem solving as often as possible. They will be encouraged to work independently and to work in groups as members of research teams. Such challenges are stimulating and they develop skills and techniques that are vital for future careers. The emphasis will be upon shared learning.

11 We will make full use of our links with the industrial and business community. These support learning in the curriculum and through the SMSC (Spiritual, Moral, Social and Cultural) programme. Staff are encouraged to develop links with employers to ensure that they maintain up-to-date knowledge of at least one aspect of the world of work outside the school. Wherever possible we will make the curriculum as relevant and real as possible. The principle is to make these experiences as active and interactive as possible.

12 We will use all the resources in our community to help students to learn. Active visits from specialists are stimulating and informative and will be used frequently.

13 We believe that it is important to set each student relevant and well-structured tasks to complete in a reasonable time. Such tasks are discussed first, methods are analysed together and students are encouraged to share in self-evaluation so that they can help to assess their progress with their teachers.

14 We believe that these methods will best be expressed in a modular-based curriculum. This means that each student will be asked to work on tasks that have a clear structure with a short-term goal. This injects rigour, pace and a keen sense of achievement into the curriculum. Our modules will be in six-week units and parents will receive reports at the end of each unit.

The details of what is involved in enabling teachers to create a modular learning culture at another secondary school has been expressed in the following document.

Modular Culture

Or

Developing Autonomous Learners

GUIDANCE FOR STAFF

WHY MODULAR LEARNING?

Modular learning provides students with short-term goals which increases student motivation. It also enables teachers and students to maximise use of ICT in teaching and learning. This will be enhanced by regular feedback to students and parents on attainment and progress in each module.

Modular learning should involve the identification of clear learning outcomes which are shared with students at the beginning of each module and which are based on the motivational force of regular feedback. Subject areas will build their curriculum progressively across the year and key stage through modular curriculum.

Modular learning will involve subject teachers and learning tutors engaging in a dialogue with students about their learning. This will take the form of setting clear targets for learning and giving regular feedback on previous performance and targets. Modular learning ties in with the half-termly (every six weeks) reporting system and revised academic year structure in operation at the school. The learning tutor discusses progress with each student and agrees learning targets for the next module. Parents will be invited to school in order to discuss progress at the start of every new module.

Tutors and students maintain an overview of module grades and these are monitored by pastoral and subject staff in order to identify trends, which may require reinforcement or intervention.

THE MODULAR PROCESS

Each module follows the same process and requires the teacher to take a specific attitude to the student in order to maximise the benefit to the learner. It is made up of three parts:

- Planning
- Teaching and learning
- Assessment and reporting.

PLANNING

At the start of the module, the teacher outlines the content for the next six weeks and the learning goals. This may be paper-based, digital, oral or a combination, but students must be clear about their learning objectives.

There should then follow a discussion of the possible teaching and learning strategies that can be used to make the knowledge accessible to and then understood by the students. This discussion will be limited with Year 7 students but should be detailed with Year 11 and post 16 students.

If the department is not using a standard assessment for the end of that module then the way the learning is to be assessed should also be discussed. For example, the grade could consist of the average marks from all the classwork and homework, it could be the assessment of a single long assignment handed in at the end of the unit. It might even be a piece of video or an audio tape on occasion.

The process so far should have taken no more than one lesson and is something akin to writing the lesson plans for the next six weeks.

TEACHING AND LEARNING

The teaching and learning of the curriculum material begins next and this will follow the guidelines agreed with the class during the first lesson. A significant number of milestones and checkpoints are needed if the module is to be studied using a learner-centred approach. The teacher will deliver a number of significant lecture and Q & A sessions during most modules, regardless of the amount of research-based learning that is happening. Students need direction as well as creative space; getting the balance between the two is important.

ASSESSMENT AND REPORTING

This process allows review of work and reflection on learning.

At the end of the module the assessment requires one lesson and should involve:

- all work to have been marked
- grades to be discussed with student and understood

- progress towards targets to be discussed
- new targets agreed for the next six weeks
- grades to be given for attainment and progress and comments to be written on the report, if needed
- student to write down new targets
- form tutor to collate grades and comments with students and to discuss progress
- prioritise new targets for next module
- form tutor to write comments as necessary on report
- student to write comments on report as necessary
- report is taken home by student
- parents sign to acknowledge and write any comments they wish to add.

The design delivery of all modules must share some common features and processes. How subject areas choose to do this is a matter for each department. Modular learning is not a paper based system and need not involve any extra paper-work.

The key components of the modular curriculum which must feature in all modular learning are summarised below and given in detail overleaf.

Guidance for students on the module

Guidance for teachers on the module

Differentiation of work in modular learning

Curriculum enhancement, ICT, EUI and industry

Module tasks

Shared assessment criteria in student friendly language

Feedback to students on performance in each module and target setting using process similar to those involved in the school learning contract.

A STUDENT GUIDE

This is a summary for the student giving an overview or map indicating to students what the module will involve and what they will learn.

The module map will give an overview of:

- The ways in which students will learn in the module.

- The activities they will engage in.
- The kinds of work or evidence that they will produce.

Students should be given this information at the start of a module, but this need not be paper based.

Departments could:

- issue a module map as a one page outline at the start of the module
- simply tell students how the module will work, as long as the outline contains the points above
- write an outline of the module on the student learning contract which departments could issue at the start of a module if they choose to use this.

Whichever method is used, students must be clear at the outset about the contents of the module, the key activities and the expected learning outcomes.

TEACHER GUIDE

It is vital that all staff delivering a module have a common understanding of what is involved. A simple teacher guide can achieve this. The guidance given need not be paper based, it could be given verbally at a department meeting (if guidance is issued at a meeting this should be briefly included in minutes).

Guidance for teachers should include:

- An overview of where the module fits into the overall programme (where it fits into year and key stage plan).
- Highlighting of National Curriculum programme of study coverage
- Highlighting of key assessment opportunities – which activities are essential for students to do in order to demonstrate achievement, which level descriptors are covered?
- Reference to stimulus materials available, including departmental resources such as fact sheets, worksheets, texts, ICT resources, etc.
- Access to equipment, including ICT.
- Access to other resources.
- Advice on how to run the assignment, including advice on homework.
- Indication on the kinds of tasks and activities that should be given.
- Deadlines for completion and assessment.

Key questions to ask here include: 'Has the department produced a key stage plan in order to ensure that the modules produced do not lead to a disjointed curriculum and does each module fit into it progressively?'

DIFFERENTIATION

Modules should recognise that students of different abilities may require differentiated contexts, language and presentation of materials. This is particularly so for students in different bands in Key Stage 3.

Differentiation may be reflected in different:

- information presented
- tasks and questions set
- supporting stimulus
- deadlines.

In some modules or parts of modules, all students will do the same things. Other activities will require support, consolidation and extension material for use by different groups of students.

Three levels of materials should be produced where it is appropriate for students to do different things (that is, where appropriate, not for every piece of work). These could, for example, be organised as covering three bands of national curriculum levels, or alternatively, as providing consolidation of new learning for some, extension to new learning for others and going over previously covered material for students in difficulty.

Key questions to ask here include:

- Does the module contain material which is appropriate for students of different ability?
- If the module is in use for North and South bands, in what ways will differences in ability be recognised? (Not by outcome in all cases!)
- If different provision is made, is it by differentiated contexts, language, presentation or other?

CURRICULUM ENHANCEMENT

Modules should reflect the school's curriculum priorities including:

- ICT integrated in a progressive way

- Industry Links

- Economic and Industrial Understanding (EIU).

All of these need not be evident in every module, but across the year and key stage there should be clear evidence of the school's added dimensions.

Key questions for departments to ask here are:

- Is there significant evidence of the school's added dimensions? If not, how can these be incorporated?

- What is the picture for delivery of these elements across the year and key stage?

- Are the school's dimensions built on progressively? Check ICT and/or EIU/Industry Co-ordinator.

MODULE TASKS

These can take a wide variety of forms. Whatever form these take they should at some point require students to:

- reproduce evidence of achievement for assessment

- produce evidence which is valid, reliable and sufficient for National Curriculum coverage

- do tasks which are appropriate for homework.

A wide variety of tasks are appropriate for modular learning, including open-ended projects, essays, tests, a collection of smaller pieces of works including homeworks etc. Not all assessment need be written assessment. Some could be oral presentation, video or audio-tape, computer aided, multi-media etc.

It is important that discussion of the teaching and learning methods are discussed with the class at the beginning of the module. The first lesson thus becomes a joint lesson planning session with the class. The students help you to write your lesson plans for the next six weeks. The involvement of the students in this process increases the older they get.

ASSESSMENT CRITERIA

Modules are motivating because they provide short-term targets. A key part in creating this motivational gain is in students knowing in advance how they will be judged.

Modules should make clear to students exactly how they will be assessed.

This can be explained at the start of the module, or be given during the module, or be on a piece of paper.

Every student should be able to go about his or her work knowing in advance precisely what is required to achieve a particular level or grade.

Some departments choose to make students familiar with generic grade criteria (A-E, for example), others write grade criteria in the context of tasks set. The precise method is up to the department to choose.

Review points should be built into modules at particular tasks, especially significant tasks requiring students to review their work done with the teacher.

Depending on the results of the review, a student may progress onto tasks at a higher or lower level of difficulty or return to the previous task using support or consolidation materials. Review points are therefore crossover points where students may change level and go on to use different materials. Review points provide the opportunity to upgrade or adjust student work based on their performance.

TUTORING AND FEEDBACK TO STUDENTS

Subject teachers should provide feedback to students on their performance at the end of each module. Some departments do this very effectively using the school's learning contract. The contract is issued at the start of the module outlining what the student will learn and how he or she will be assessed. At the end of the module the teacher assesses the work and writes comments.

Students also write comments on how they performed and together, students and teachers agree learning targets for the next module. The contracts can also be taken home to show parents in order to provide more feedback.

Departments need not use the learning contract, but where it is not used a similar process to the above involving student/teacher review must be carried out.

Students will then take their reports around to each subject area in the last two weeks of a module. Subject teachers will then grade module performance for:

- progress
- attainment.

Teachers will make a brief comment at least once per academic year (in practice most write comments two or three times) when they feel it is appropriate. There should be discussion with students about performance allowing reflection and review to be carried out. Students should be encouraged to challenge the grades and negotiate with your new learning targets.

Tutors will complete the review and will comment once per term.

Based on a review of module grades tutors will briefly set targets for improvement in particular subjects.

Subject teachers can monitor who has been set targets by simply asking students at the start of each module who has had targets set for that subject.

Directors of Student Services will sample tutor module tracking sheets during each module in order to identify trends or issues needing intervention. Tutors should also identify these and involve the Director.

The modular process helps the culture because it forces specific habits to be developed.

It demands new approaches to teaching.

It provides formalised, regular assessment and therefore monitoring.

It means that no student can develop learning problems for more than six weeks without being detected.

Summary

Our intention is that, at the end of this chapter, you will have:

- gained a fundamental understanding of the importance of the relationship of the learning culture to educational attainment
- realised that teaching is as much about changing the attitude of mind towards learning as imparting information
- understood that giving staff greater ownership of the teaching and students greater ownership of their learning are important steps to changing the learning culture
- learnt that the modular culture is a known route to creating a successful learning culture
- realised that short-term tasks, review and reflection at regular intervals are important aspects of learning.

Vision and philosophy

Introduction

Whatever text you read about leadership the first thing it always says is: 'ensure you have a clear vision that you can communicate to others'. This is not something that you can buy in a shop, learn from a text or which you can acquire from a series of lectures. Your vision and philosophy will be wrought from your principles and the buffeting you get from trying to put them into practice in your daily life. Any Ofsted report and commentary about highly successful schools invariably starts with a reference to the vision of the school and the leader and the clear way he or she transmits this to others in the organisation.

How do you get your vision?

First of all you have to know what you passionately believe in.

TASK 15

Demonstration

Prepare an answer to the following question. If you were to join a demonstration and get involved in direct action, for what cause would you be stirred enough to go out and join a march?

This is a question I always ask prospective senior leaders and deputies at interview. It is designed to find out what motivates you in life and what principles are really dear to you. If your answer is trite or it takes some time to give a response, it suggests that you do not have clearly thought out principles or that you do not passionately believe, or, better, have faith, in anything at all.

Until you genuinely know what really stirs you to action and which ideas you passionately believe in, you are not ready for headship in our current turbulent times. Passion is not taught but nurtured through tough experiences. The following questions read as a banal litany of conscience-pricking social ideas and provocative argument. They are likely to make you feel strongly either for or against them because of their stupidity.

Do you really care that so many people in this country live below the poverty line?

Of course you do, we all do, it is a 'natural reaction'. We all want to eliminate poverty and if someone ever says you don't care about poor people you get incensed. However, a person or family is defined as poor in this country if the income in the household is less than half the average national wage. So, under this definition is it possible ever to find a way of eradicating poverty? We could say though that, in all probability, by the standards of 1900, no person in this country is really poor in material terms. In fact, if they are, it is almost a matter of choice because support is available from the welfare state. So why perhaps should we bother too much about it?

Some more questions about morality and ethics:

Which aspect of the argument makes you committed, angry or frustrated?

- Do you think that our welfare state helps people out of poverty or does it encourage a dependency culture?

- What is wrong with selective education? What is right about selective education?

- How does comprehensive education really benefit young people?

- Does it matter that you do not know and understand the second law of thermodynamics?

- Does it matter that you have not read/watched and studied Hamlet?

- Do you accept that the last two questions are essential ingredients in the education of any teacher today?

- Do you have an answer to the question 'Why are we here?'

- Have you ever thought about it and come up with an answer, however banal?

- When a decision is difficult, how do you reach an answer that you are convinced is right and that is not said just to please or placate your audience?

- Do you have a soul/spirit/ eternal being that exists above and beyond you, or are you just a collection of atoms and molecules joined together in a particular way?

For some people there are no right and wrong answers to the above questions, but to others most have specific answers that they are certain are 'true' or correct. It is not suggested that you take up any perspective suggested by the questions, however, you should have felt your blood boil at some of the questions and arguments and been really frustrated by, or dismissive of, others!

——————— Identifying your beliefs ———————

TASK 16

Discovering your philosophy

Examine your soul, your conscience and your past? What actions, words and thoughts are you most proud of and of which are you most ashamed?

Which of the great philosophies of the world have you read?

Which do you most admire?

What of the great religions of the world do you know and which have resonance in your heart?

Where are you on your personal faith journey in life?

There are no 'right' answers that are the same for all of us, but there are basic tenets and moral values on which all of our societies are based. As a leader of a school community in that society your personal philosophy cannot be too different from that which is acceptable to your community represented by the governing body. If it is, you will need to examine why and then do something about it. If you cannot reconcile your own personal faith with that of the governors then changing jobs might be something to consider.

Consider what really matters – religious values, moral values, humanism or whatever. You have to go and find it. When you have found it/them, make sure they are principles and not values. Principles should stand the test of time and 'the slings and arrows of outrageous fortune' but values tend to change with experience. Find out, learn and live the difference between the two.

It is suggested that reading *First things first* by Covey and Merrill, if you are not already familiar with it, could help you to focus on your principles and help to decide what is valuable. If you espouse a philosophy or religion, re-examine its basic truths and reaffirm your personal faith.

When you have developed in your own mind your principles of life, find a way to put them into words and to summarise them in a succinct phrase or sentence. You need to be very comfortable with yourself. This then becomes your 'motto'.

TASK 17

Further understanding your personal values

What, if you are writing your own obituary, do you want to be remembered for? Write down a paragraph or two about yourself that you would like read out at your memorial service. Repeat the exercise every few years, making sure you are comfortable with it. Again, test it with your mentor or partner.

So now you are comfortable with the picture you hold of yourself and it is not too different from the way others perceive you. Ideally, but rarely, it is the same.

_____ Applying your philosophy in leadership _____

Now move on to schools and education.

TASK 18

The ideal school

Can you visualise the ideal organisation or school you wish to be leading? Write a brief description of what it would be like. Confine yourself to no more than two sides of A4. Show it to a friend/mentor/colleague. Discuss it, challenge the assumptions and refine it. This becomes your ideal!

Next start working out in your mind how you will try to get from where you are to where you want to be. Try to work out the sort of actions and plans you need to put in place in order to help you along the way. One of the most helpful strategies for turning ideas into real action plans is described by Brent Davies and Linda Ellison in their book *Strategic Direction and Development of the School*. They develop a model of planning which goes in three steps from the ideal to the immediate practical tasks. They use the concepts of 'Futures Thinking' for ideals and visions for where you would hope to be in ten years' time. From these, strategic intent and plans for delivery in three to five years are derived, and finally, action or operational plans and targets are developed for the next 12 to 18 months. We will look at these in detail in Chapter 7.

So now your 'passion for education' is contained in clear statements and plans. How do you transmit it?

At every opportunity make sure that you let your audience know where you stand and what counts. Know your audience and tailor the message to suit each one but without compromising principles.

You have to learn to live your ideas in everything you do. Try to eliminate actions that cause confusion and which conflict with your vision. Keep on returning to the vision in your mind. A relentless pursuit of it is required!

CASE STUDY

Table 5.1 below is example of the mission statement, aims and objectives of a school.

It contains most of the basic statements and tenets that are expected of a school, but notice that its mission statement talks about the future of the school as a network, which suggests a different form of organisation from the normal. Although only one word, it shows that considerable thought has gone into the writing of the mission statement, as this is obviously a radical departure from the current norm.

TABLE 5.1 Mission statement

MISSION

The school is creating a quality learning network that achieves excellence in all its services in an enterprising culture and in partnership with the community.

Motto:

Act Enterprisingly, Work in Partnership, Achieve Excellence

AIM	OBJECTIVE
1 To nurture the academic, personal and moral development of every child in our care.	1.1 To emphasise individuality and individual responsibility.
2 To promote the *pursuit of excellence* and achievement by each student of their abilities and skills to their maximum potential.	2.1 To recognise that each student has different aspirations and to develop them.

AIM	OBJECTIVE
	2.2 To encourage students to believe in themselves and to have *high expectations and high standards.*
	2.3 To encourage students to care for themselves, their family and their *community.*
3 To create and maintain an *ethos* which encourages *excellence, self-reliance, co-operation, enthusiasm and initiative.*	3.1 To create a positive learning culture amongst all students.
	3.2 To provide a wide range of studies, sports, cultural and extra-curricular activities.
	3.3 To provide all students with a progressive programme of *problem solving and enterprise activities.*
	3.4 To provide all students with direct experience of the workplace and *extensive work experience.*
4 To deliver the national curriculum with enhanced mathematics, sciences and technology fostering direct links with industry and commerce.	4.1 The curriculum must stimulate and challenge in the most appropriate structure for learning.
	4.2 To *involve industry and commerce* in all aspects of school life.
5 To develop *aesthetic values* in all our students.	5.1 To value the arts as highly as the sciences and technology.
	5.2 To value the role of the arts in a civilised society.
6 To establish the school as a learning organisation for the *community of East Dartford.*	6.1 To build close *partnerships* between students, parents, teachers and individuals in business and the local community.
	6.2 To provide educational and recreational opportunities for the community.

AIM	OBJECTIVE
7 To prepare students for life in the wider *European Community* and beyond.	7.1 To give an insight into the contribution made by the many different racial and ethnic groups to our civilisation.
	7.2 To ensure that all students can communicate in at least one foreign language and that they have a sound knowledge of our European heritage and culture.
8 To keep the school at the forefront of *technological change*	8.1 To maximise the use of technology in teaching and learning.
	8.2 To be a centre for *educational research and development*.
9 To establish a reputation *for innovation and success.*	9.1 To establish the school as a *world class* learning organisation.

OBJECTIVES

To bring about the cultural change needed to achieve our long-term aims and objectives we will establish more immediate objectives, methods and evaluation procedures.

1 We will maintain the strong philosophy in the school which is based upon the principles of enterprise, partnership and the pursuit of excellence. We will teach clear moral and spiritual values. We will encourage our students to care for one another and to establish a caring community. These values will be defined in each tutor group, year group and house and we will do our best to ensure that they are understood and practised.

2 We will maintain a civilised community. In this way it will be our objective to teach students about their responsibilities not only to the community in which they live, but also the wider community in Europe and beyond. It is very much an objective to help young people to understand those forces which help to civilise mankind. Consequently we will study the history of different societies and we will to encourage our students to understand the rich contribution that has been made to our culture by different racial and ethnic groups.

3 It is our objective to give a rich and broad education to our students as well as providing the enhanced scientific and technological education that will be so important to them in the future. We aim to make our students good communicators. We want them to read widely and appreciate literature and poetry. In all this it is an objective to ensure that each individual develops his or her talents. It is a clear objective to ensure that our students are taught at the correct pace to enable them to achieve the best possible progress.

4 It is our objective to establish a curriculum that contains skills, values, concepts and experiences that give our students a defined and clear opportunity to make progress as they go through school. It is our objective to develop a cohesive education and to underpin much of our work with clear problem-solving and individualised learning methods that will enable our students to think independently and to have a spirit of enquiry.

5 It is our objective to provide the best possible technological systems to support the curriculum and to ensure that learning takes place in the most lively, stimulating and demanding environment. We aim to ensure that our students will have the confidence to make the fullest use of the technological challenges facing them in our modern society.

6 It is our objective to provide a rigorous and stimulating aesthetic education. We believe that music, the expressive arts and the performing arts should play an important part in the life of every student in the school. The value and contribution that these activities make to each of us cannot be underestimated.

7 It is our objective to ensure that our students are properly prepared for the world of work and for their life after school. They should have not only the appropriate skills but also an enterprising attitude and an enquiring mind. They will achieve this by being involved in a coherent programme of work-related problem-solving activities and relevant work experience. We will also place a strong emphasis upon understanding of self, upon an understanding of nutrition, healthy living, good diet and good personal relationships.

8 It is our objective to ensure that all our students acquire interests and involvement in activities that would keep them healthy and confident in the increased leisure time that they will face in the future.

9 It is our objective to develop the character of the individuals in our care and it is an objective to encourage the students to take responsibility for their own learning, to evaluate their own progress and to take them through the pain barrier that often exists before they can achieve their objectives. It is our belief that shared tasks and objectives will help students have a sense of purpose throughout their time at school.

10 It is our objective to create as seamless as possible the transition between school and the adult world. It is our intention to make the interface between the school and the outside world as transparent as possible by creating a culture and environment in the school as close to the adult world as possible, particularly for our post-16 students.

Summary

Our intention is that, at the end of this chapter, you will have:

- realised the importance of having a personal faith in helping to develop your vision
- learnt that your philosophy of life and education have been developed by your experience
- gained the confidence in yourself and your philosophy to give you the courage to express it and live it in your daily life
- understood that creating a philosophy and motto for your school, if they do not exist, will involve all the community
- come to understand that it is necessary to re-examine your vision regularly.

chapter six

Teaching and learning

This is the core business! The curriculum and the way it is delivered are the heart of the school. The day to day delivery of the curriculum must embody the vision. The assessment recording and reporting must embody the vision. The first part of this chapter considers these issues and relates them to the Ofsted processes relating to standards and measurable outcomes. The second part of this chapter considers the way we teach and learn and considers the impact of our increased understanding of the brain and how we can accelerate and improve our learning and thinking. Also considered are types of intelligence and the need to link our teaching and learning programmes to them. Finally the importance of emotional intelligence on all aspects of education is suggested.

Managing the curriculum

In most cases you inherit a curriculum which you modify over time. However, it is good practice to imagine that you have a blank piece of paper, or more probably, a blank computer timetable program. How do you want to fill it in? What subjects should be offered? How much time should each lesson be? And so on ... Do you have answers to all these and many more myriad questions about curriculum and timetable? It is these which govern the day and make staff and student lives more or less frustrating.

Normally when you become a Head or leader of the organisation, you inherit an existing structure, process and way of living. Decisions about how much change you bring to everyone's daily life need careful consideration and need to be integrated with the themes of Chapters 2–5. However, when taking up the post of Head it is very important to know answers to all these questions because they provide long-term goals for you personally and are the embodiment of your vision in everyday life. So take time over the next task and discuss your ideas with others.

TASK 19

Ideal education

On your blank piece of actual or electronic paper, consider the following ideals. Each ideal should be directly linked in your mind to your vision of education.

Here is a suggested list:

- ideal curriculum – balance between academic and vocational
- ideal day – length of lessons, amount of tutor time, should all lessons be of the same length?
- ideal year – as now; four or five terms; a fixed year of six equal units of time; any other?
- ideal size – 200, 500, 1000, …
- ideal structure
- ideal staffing arrangements
- ideal class arrangements
- ideal assessment period.

Now some questions:

- How much formal teaching?
- How much peer-to-peer learning?
- How much reflection time, target setting and discussion?
- What reporting process will you use?
- Do you want bells to indicate the start and end of lessons?
- Where does technology fit in?
- What use of the Internet and distance learning will you make?
- What use will you make of accelerated learning strategies and will you teach thinking skills?
- Do you accept the concept of multiple intelligences and, if so, how can the curriculum reflect this?
- Emotional intelligence is increasingly accepted as a concept that needs to be reflected in our education system. How should it fit in?
- Where do learning support strategies fit in?

When you have thought about your ideals try to link them together and consider them along with the questions that are posed. From this develop what you consider to be your ideal curriculum and learning framework. It will pay to do this during a quiet period, (are there any?) such as one of the holiday periods, as an extended time for deep reflection. It is difficult to do between appointment and the starting date as Head, but this is an ideal time to try to do this exercise. The difficulty is that there are so many other changes happening at this time, both internally and externally, that it is difficult to create the inner calm and reflectiveness needed. Nonetheless, when it is done in depth this exercise will help to produce an outcome that you have confidence in.

You are creating the ideal embodiment of your vision. Forget the National Curriculum, forget Ofsted, create your own ideal school. Of course, it cannot be created exactly, but as you meet reality you temper your ideal and always have this as a benchmark against which to develop the school. If you are fortunate enough to be setting up a new school then you do have the luxury to think in such a way and then to bring it as close as possible to reality. Even if you are not leading a new school, the importance of going back to first principles on this most important task cannot be overstated. It is a practice that can be very valuable and informative whenever you try to tackle any difficult problem you are trying to solve. When there is so much change and innovation happening, we constantly need to ask fundamental questions about change, but also about what we are currently doing. We need to make sure that our own personal fundamentals are not compromised unnecessarily.

We cannot continue to impose change after change on our schools without giving up some of the things we are currently doing. The capacity to ask the questions 'Why are we doing this?' and 'Of what benefit is this task to students learning today?' are very important. This approach needs to become part of the culture of the staff. In fact the capacity to have a reflective approach is important in all we do.

It is the job of the Head to ensure that the curriculum fits with the school's vision as espoused in the governors' curriculum policy statement. Check this statement and make sure that your curriculum does still fit. Bring your ideal into line as much as possible with this. We have spent far too little time on the value of reflection, whether it be as part of a learning process or part of the planning and review cycle.

Modular curriculum

Details of the modular curriculum are given in Chapter 4, *Creating a Learning Culture*, in the section *The modular culture*. The modular curriculum is a way of teaching and learning and a whole cultural approach to delivering the curriculum. It is strongly suggested that you reread this section and consider again within that context the ideal curriculum you have just created.

One of its powerful learning strategies is that reflection on what has been learned is a formal part of the learning process every six weeks. If you are in a primary school, make sure that full account of literacy and numeracy programmes has been taken and that there is sufficient time allowed for all the specialist subjects. With the increasing focus on inclusiveness and removing the barrier between Key Stage 2 and Key Stage 3 it is quite possible to get specialist expertise from your local secondary school. It is also quite possible to gain access to this specialism via video conference links and electronic links. Perhaps by 2002 it will be the norm for these links to exist.

At secondary level make sure due consideration at Key Stage 4 is given to vocational courses. Part 1 GNVQs are an increasingly popular option for all students at this level and ensuring vocational courses have equal status with academic ones is vital for their success. How much, if any, of the curriculum in your school is on-line? Do you have plans to make it so? Traditional, i.e. academic, teaching and learning do not translate easily to the new medium, however, vocational courses do.

CASE STUDY

A school that started offering GNVQ courses as alternatives to the one-year post 16 retread GCSE courses now has more students studying GNVQs post 16 than A levels in a sixth form of more than 200 students. This has been achieved, says the Head, because of the vision of a number of members of staff who saw the potential of vocational courses. It is fair to say that vocational education in this school has complete parity with A levels. This has happened because Advanced GNVQs were introduced in a wide range of subjects as the next step. Then, as soon as Part 1 GNVQs were available, they were introduced in the same subjects as the advanced courses. The next and crucial decision was to make a vocational column in the options programme for Year 10, so that all students had to take at least one Part 1 GNVQ in Years 10 and 11. The impact of this has been to ensure that all students learn GNVQ ways, which they then start applying to the more traditional GCSE courses. The teachers, too, start to change the way they deliver their lessons and learning begins to happen differently. So when it comes to a choice at post 16, students and parents have come to value the vocational courses and are happy to see their daughters and sons choosing courses such as Advanced GNVQ Science and Advanced GNVQ Art and Design. This has been helped by students who have gained good degrees at universities having gained all their advanced qualifications at school as GNVQs returning to the area.

Interestingly, the task-based learning and problem-solving approach that is used in vocational courses is much more suited to independent learning which is so important in today's world. It is also more easily adapted to learning on the Internet. Andy Rosenfield, one of the founders of the new Net University – Cardean University – states:

> 'The thing the Internet does least well is parrot the classroom, but we don't think that is a key part of education. The key part is making people do, think, interact with each other, ask questions, and form groups and we think the Internet is ideal for that.'

The need in developing the most suitable curriculum in the most suitable 'classroom' has never been more important and the traditional curriculum has never been under so much threat. Make sure that your ideal learning arrangements derived from Task 19 take proper account of vocational and on-line learning.

———— Assessment ————

If the learning culture has been created properly then assessment, recording and reporting, will have been an integral part of the structure and it is only necessary to emphasise the importance of integrating the curriculum, the culture and assessment.

CASE STUDY

Below is an example of secondary school's evaluation and review guidelines that are integrated with its curriculum and its philosophy.

Evaluation and review guidelines

We need to identify and celebrate achievement. The school's reward system is used to praise, motivate and reward students whenever their performance merits it. It seems sensible to evaluate work with our students and staff on a regular basis. The process of evaluation should become endemic and the following procedures are significant.

1 Every six weeks we will publish a Management Information Pack (MIP) containing a summary of the key quantifiable Performance Indicators in the school. The information is then analysed by senior staff and governors and the school's performance is compared to that set out in the School Development Plan. Actions are then taken where necessary, particularly praise, but also corrective measures.

2 Departments review the curriculum at regular meetings throughout the year. Staff work closely with the head of department to ensure that schemes of work are relevant, that the timing is efficient and that the pace is appropriate for the students in their care.

3 Every member of staff sets and marks homework regularly.

4 We have a clear communication system with parents to ensure rapid communication if work is not being done effectively or if students behave in an anti-social way.

5 We use cognitive ability and other tests (MIDYIS, YELLIS, ALIS) to identify the potential of every student. We use this data to establish benchmarks and targets through the school's Value Added process. This enables us to have an additional guideline to see if students are underperforming. All students have planners/day books that they are encouraged to complete meticulously. They are signed each week by parents and teachers.

6 Pastoral managers and tutors regularly analyse students' diaries and planners to encourage and support study patterns.

7 Heads of Department, Pastoral Managers and senior staff regularly analyse the work of a sample of students each term (six weeks) and discuss their progress with them.

8 All students from year 10 upward have a mentor who is a senior member of staff. They meet them once a term on average. This enables an additional level of monitoring and academic support to be provided for students.

9 Reports are compiled every six weeks at the end of each module. Grades are given for attainment and progress and a comment is written when necessary. Records of Achievement/Progress files are maintained by students from year to year and are finalised in Year 11 with enhancements in Years 12 and 13.

10 The work of those students who need special support is monitored by the Co-ordinator of Special Needs, who also looks after the interests of special needs children in the various departments.

11 All departments review their curriculum and Development Plans annually and set new targets and goals. We have introduced an internal audit process and will encourage neighbouring heads of department to review and evaluate progress and effectiveness. There is an annual whole school review.

12 The leadership and management of the school are reviewed regularly using the MIP. The Senior Leadership Team evaluates them. The governors share in this evaluation.

13 Staff and parents will be invited to become involved in this evaluation.

Use of technology

In today's world the impact of the digital age on every aspect of life has already been profound. Business has re-engineered itself and rebuilt itself from the bottom up to ensure that the relevant processes properly reflect the most efficient and effective way of achieving their organisations' ends. In education we have only just begun. There is a whole chapter (Chapter 10) on the impact of technology on the work of the Head, but when considering how to manage the curriculum today it cannot be done without considering how you will want to use technology. It is almost possible to conceive of any arrangement for delivering the curriculum because there will be technology that can be used to achieve it. Cost and sustainability are, as ever, the two limiting factors. Nonetheless costs are coming down so rapidly that even if you cannot afford the technology today you most certainly will be able to tomorrow. Thus when you are planning curriculum and associated structural changes, future-proofing the change, although impossible, has to be considered and decisions taken that show due regard to these factors.

TASK 20

Ideal technology-supported learning

If you had access to the best technology that you can think of, how would you structure classes in your school?

Consider:

- retaining the status quo

- incorporating whiteboard interactive technology in each classroom

- video-links to all rooms in your school and to all homes if needed so that live and recorded lessons can be viewed and treated interactively.

All of the above could currently be made available if you can afford it. Tomorrow we will be able to afford it. Did you come up with the same answers that you wrote for your ideal curriculum earlier? Does the new structure fit with your vision? There are no easy answers but you are the Head and you have to decide!

——— Ofsted processes ———

One of the most important factors, but least admired, in the improvement of school standards in all schools has been brought about by Ofsted. It is interesting to note that although the inspection process gets very poor ratings within the profession and from the media, in a survey conducted among Heads over 80 per cent were very satisfied with the process and felt it had had a positive effect on raising standards in their schools.

If you are not already familiar with the inspection process then it is imperative that you take time to understand the *process*. There will almost certainly be a copy of the *Handbook for Ofsted Inspections* in the school. Check that it is the latest edition, then use it to identify the essential educational monitoring processes and build these into the quality assurance and monitoring strategies of the school.

There are seven key areas that need monitoring:

- high expectations and achievement
- lesson planning
- teaching methods and strategies
- pupil management/discipline
- management of time and resources
- assessment and reporting procedures
- homework.

If these processes become the normal way of life for all staff then monitoring ceases to be an issue and so to does the visit of Ofsted, since the inspectors will only be following the procedures that everyone uses on a daily basis.

TASK 21

Preparing for Ofsted inspection

Study the Ofsted inspection process and decide:

1 What documents you would need to prepare for an inspection.

2 How you would manage the process in your school, not just for one week, but as a process that is continuous throughout the year.

Multiple intelligences and accelerated learning

In recent years there has been an enormous improvement in our understanding of the brain and how we learn. The work on neuroscience, different forms of intelligence and thinking skills has started to have a considerable impact on pedagogy. Combine this understanding with the dramatic increase in our ability to access information and we in school have to examine radically what is the most effective way of delivering academic and vocational learning to our students. We also need to consider the other aspects of education – the socialisation of young people – which we do in a more haphazard way. The question we have to consider is 'If we change the traditional school day and subject mix, will we still be able to deliver the other skills by the same route as now?' No one knows the answer. But before we try to take the next step, we have to maintain an environment in which young people feel supported and where the atmosphere is supportive of learning, i.e. a disciplined and defined environment where young people have high expectations and have ownership of their own learning. That is why the three fundamentals of a good school have to be secure before any change is attempted.

 TASK 22

Intelligences in the curriculum

Make yourself familiar with Howard Gardner's work on multiple intelligences and that of Daniel Goleman on emotional intelligence. We suggested earlier that you read them, so you may already be familiar with them.

1 Write a short summary of each type of intelligence for circulation to all your staff.

2 Ask the staff to examine their curriculum and to find ways to ensure that the teaching and learning in each subject area make use of all types of intelligence.

Recent work on the neurology of the brain has given us more understanding than ever about how the brain works, thus telling us more than ever before about how we learn and how we think. Our understanding should allow us to devise the best teaching and learning strategies.

Styles of teaching and learning

1 Talk and listen.

2 Talk and talk: debate and discussion.

3 Question and answer, teacher-led or student-led.

4 Reading.

5 Writing.

6 Pictures and shapes, including spider diagram flow charts and fishbone diagrams.

7 Numbers and symbols.

8 Practical working – learning by doing.

9 Making summary notes.

TASK 23

Learning styles

1 Do you know which learning style suits you best? Find out which methods you use best by trying out each method on different pieces of work, or you may be able to work it out by reflecting on previous studies and examination periods. You could also ask close and longstanding friends for their views on how you learn best.

2 Decide how much impact the range of intelligences that individuals show can make to the achievement of the students and how much value to place on them with the staff.

3 Decide what the key learning styles are and how you can make staff aware of theirs. Having made them aware of their own style you then need to work out how to develop strategies to identify learning styles among students.

What setting arrangements will you have – are you aiming to have an accelerated group? As stated many times throughout, the expectations you have of students' ability, constantly communicated to the staff so that they too have very high expectations, is one of the most sure ways of raising standards. If an accelerated group is created it focuses the minds of all the students, the staff and the parents on who should be in that group and what the criteria are for entry. This automatically creates an attitude of mind that promotes achievement. Not only will those students who are selected for this group have higher expectations, if managed properly, many others will say if he or she can get into that group, then so can I. Whatever strategy is chosen it is essential to create a positive learning culture, one that says, 'It's cool to learn'.

Thinking skills

The goal of all teaching has always been to get students to think. There are many different thinking skills courses on the market and texts that describe them. It is suggested that you carry out a search on the Internet to find a good reference selection from which to choose. Edward de Bono has spent a lifetime developing thinking skills and is much admired and respected right around the world. It is disappointing that his work does not have as much prominence in his own country. His work on Lateral Thinking, Six Thinking Hats and his CORT Thinking Strategies are outstanding and the courses that introduce these to staff and students will pay enormous dividends. They will help not just in teaching in the classroom, but at meetings, councils, for revision and planning sessions and to minimise argument and tension.

Six thinking hats

De Bono identifies six major ways of thinking. These are shown in Table 6.1 below.

TABLE 6.1 Six Thinking Hats

- White Hat — Information finding and handling
- Red Hat — Use of your feelings – how do feel about an issue?
- Black Hat — Cautious thinking or negative thinking – what is wrong with this, why shouldn't we do it, why can't we do it?
- Yellow Hat — Positive thinking, consider benefits
- Green Hat — Creative thinking, generating new ideas
- Blue Hat — Cool and detached, managing the thinking

The colour of the thinking mode relates to its general meaning. Restricting thinking in an activity to one colour type at a time is very powerful and can sharpen and shorten meetings and discussions.

Effective teaching

Hay Mcber have recently reported on the effective teacher. They found three factors within the teacher's control that significantly influence pupil progress:

- teaching skills
- professional characteristics
- classroom climate.

They define teaching skills as follows.

'Those "micro-behaviours" that the effective teacher constantly exhibits when teaching a class. They include behaviours like:

- involving all pupils in the lesson
- using differentiation appropriately to challenge all pupils in the class
- using a variety of activities or learning methods
- applying teaching methods appropriate to the national curriculum objectives
- using a variety of questioning techniques to probe pupils' knowledge and understanding.'

They outline five factors that make up professional characteristics:

Professionalism

Challenge and support: A commitment to enable all pupils to be successful.

Confidence: The belief in one's ability to be effective and to take on challenges.

Creating trust: Being consistent and fair. Keeping one's word.

Respect for others: The underlying belief that individuals matter and deserve respect.

Thinking

Analytical thinking: The ability to think logically.

Conceptual thinking: The ability to see patterns and links.

Planning and setting expectations

Drive for improvement: *Relentless energy for setting and meeting challenging targets, for pupils and the school.*

Information seeking: *Intense intellectual curiosity.*

Initiative: *The drive to act now to anticipate and pre-empt events.*

Leadership

Flexibility: *The ability and willingness to adapt to the needs of a situation and change tactics.*

Holding people accountable: *The drive and ability to set clear expectations and parameters and to hold others accountable for performance.*

Managing pupils: *The drive and ability to provide clear direction to pupils, and to enthuse and motivate them.*

Passion for learning: *The drive and ability to support pupils in their learning, and to help them become confident and independent learners.*

Relating to others

Impact and influence: *The ability and drive to produce positive outcomes by impressing and influencing others.*

Teamworking: *The ability to work with others to achieve shared goals.*

Understanding others: *The drive and ability to understand others, and why they behave as they do.*

The third factor is classroom climate

'*Classroom climate is defined as the collective perceptions by pupils of what it feels like to be a pupil in any particular teacher's classroom, where those perceptions influence every student's motivation to learn and perform to the best of his or her ability.*

Each climate dimension represents an aspect of how the pupils feel in that classroom. They are defined as follows:

1 Clarity *around the purpose of each lesson.*

2 Order *within the classroom, where discipline, order and civilised behaviour are maintained.*

3 *A clear set of* Standards *as to how pupils should behave, do and achieve, with a clear focus on higher standards.*

4 Fairness: *equal treatment and consistency of rewards and punishments.*

5 Participation: *the opportunity for pupils to participate actively in class.*

6 Support: *feeling emotionally supported in the classroom, so that pupils are willing to try new things and learn from mistakes.*

7 Safety: *the classroom is a safe place, no risk from bullying, or other fear-arousing factors.*

8 Interest: *the feeling that the classroom is an interesting and exciting place to be, where pupils feel stimulated to learn.*

9 Environment: *a comfortable, well organised, clean and attractive classroom.'*

The research conducted by Hay Mcber involved many teachers and students in both the primary and secondary phase. The above summaries from the report indicate the key factors in teacher effectiveness. As the Head you have to find the combination of activities and the best strategies to maximise the effectiveness of your teachers. It is maximising these factors that enables the standards in the classroom to be raised to the highest level possible and this then provides the atmosphere and culture that leads to continuously improving standards.

TASK 24

Teaching characteristics

1 Using each of the Hay Mcber definitions, devise a strategy for implementing the most effective way of bringing each to life.

2 Now try to integrate the definitions to create a coherent whole.

3 Now check this against your vision.

———— Summary ————

Our intention is that, at the end of this chapter, you will have:

■ learnt that the curriculum in the school must embody the vision of the school

- developed your ideal curriculum to use as an important personal benchmark for a Head

- understood that the changes happening in our world today have to be reflected much more quickly in the curriculum we offer and the way we deliver it

- acquired the ability to use the Ofsted process as a very powerful continuous improvement tool

- see that there are many ways to deliver education in today's world and that vocational courses should have parity or even superiority to traditional academic courses

- become enthused to use technology to change the way we teach and learn

- found ways to incorporate multiple intelligences and emotional intelligence into the curriculum

- become aware that there are many ways that we learn and that teachers need to use the full range of teaching techniques to ensure that students can maximise their potential

- learnt that thinking skills play an important part in increasing learning potential and motivation

- acquired the expertise to develop the wide range of skills that have been identified by Hay McBer which teachers need to master to be fully effective.

Managing and leading change

Introduction

Having articulated a vision and a philosophy that give a general guidance to life, or at least having spent time considering who you are and where you might be going, the next process to begin is the creation of suitable plans that will help take your school forward and lead to sustained improvement. It is likely that considerable change will be required.

This chapter outlines some of the thinking behind planning and the process required to create next year's operational targets so that they fit in with your long-term goals. It also looks at some of the strategies to aid implementation and manage the changes.

Planning

Again, a great deal has already been written about planning and a good selection of references is easily located by using the Internet. The first task is to read some of them. Skim read until you find an author and style that suit you. A lot of what has been written about planning is too mechanistic and too prescriptive. However, when you first start it can be quite helpful to have a prescriptive methodology to follow. The advantage is that you have a recipe and following that can be quite helpful while you are learning the process and the skills. It soon becomes a disadvantage, however, because you will find that it is too limiting, and acts more like a straitjacket than a method to help you take your organisation forward.

SWOT analysis

How do you know where you and your organisation are in terms of planning?

TABLE 7.1 Questions to ask about existing plans

1 Does a plan already exist?

2 If so, how detailed is it? Does it set targets for the organisation which are achievable? Are these targets linked to measurable outcomes and do they have individuals responsible for delivering them?

3 How well do others understand it? If you asked the caretaker/assistant site manager what the key targets in the school's development plan were for the current year, would he or she be able to tell you? How many parents and students would know?

4 Is there a clear link to budgets with an audit trail that can easily be followed?

5 Is there a five year maintenance plan?

6 Does the plan set strategic targets and goals for five and ten years?

These questions form part of a SWOT analysis. Carrying out a SWOT analysis means looking at the strengths, weaknesses, opportunities and threats that exist for the school. This analysis is best done with all the staff at a suitable time during the first three months in post. Judging the correct time depends on the answers you gained to the above questions. The SWOT analysis should then be carried out in detail as a whole staff activity about once every three years. If it is done too often, it becomes a chore rather than the analytical exercise it needs to be to create maximum effect.

The development plan

Whatever stage you have reached with planning, it is all worthless unless it is owned by the staff and students and unless it is a living embodiment of the vision you and the governors hold for your school.

TASK 25

Analysis of development plan

Study your school's current plan and write down answers to the questions in Table 7.1. Next consider your own principles and vision of what a school should be and mark on the plan those aspects that are contrary to your own views.

If you are not yet a Head then decide how much you want to try to change next year's plan to incorporate your own philosophy. If you are already a Head or leader, then decide why there are some aspects of your organisation's plans with which you disagree. You will also need to decide if they can remain within the plan or whether there are in-built contradictions that you may have to live with in the short term.

A development plan is given in the final section of the book. It is the plan devised by about 100 heads and the Technology Colleges Trust to provide direction for the specialist schools movement.

———— Creating right thinking ————

The first step in creating the plan you want is to ensure that staff understand the vision of the organisation and have some idea of how to move towards achieving it. If you have had the opportunity of involving the staff in its development then they too are likely to own it, thus making the planning process that much easier. More importantly it will make the implementation of the plan and the achievement of the targets that much more likely.

If you are a new Head you need to create such an approach. When you first start in a new job there is a honeymoon period and the existing staff will want to impress you. You can test their commitment by involving them in the planning process early on and seeing how well they take on the responsibility of delivering specific targets.

There are a many texts on school development planning which explain the details of the process very well. One of the most suitable at present is *Strategic Direction and Development of the School* by Brent Davies and Linda Ellison. The authors take school planning to new levels as they introduce the concepts of *futures thinking, strategic intent and strategic plans*, as well as *operational plans and targets*. It is strongly recommended that this book should be on the reading list of any aspiring Head.

Futures thinking

This activity requires a group of people to consider, based on the vision, what the school will be like in ten years' time. Bring into the brainstorm, conducted in yellow and green hat thinking modes only (refer to Table 6.1 in Chapter 6 for a reminder if necessary), 'all the usual suspects' that have been alluded to elsewhere in the book. Some of them are listed below in Table 7.2.

TABLE 7.2 Ideas for brainstorming

- Technology – its impact on learning

- technology – its impact on the curriculum

- technology – its impact on administration

- technology – its impact on the home (for all the above technology-related issues we advise that you read Chapter 10, *The Power of Technology*)

- teacher union intransigence, not really a green hat thinking approach, but one that needs to be considered to gain an understanding of the forces of conservatism that need to be overcome

- home school movement

- restructuring of LEAs.

TASK 26

Futures thinking

With your senior team, sit down during a period of peace and quiet, probably the summer holidays, and add to the list in Table 7.2 and then brainstorm each idea. The task can be done initially on your own, it depends how well the senior team understands your vision or the confidence you have in their knowledge. If there are constraints it may pay to produce this list on your own first and ask for additions and alterations from the team. Always ask for reasons why whenever there are requests for change. Ensure that motives are clean, or acceptable at least, and that the direction of the change fits in with the vision of the school over this timeframe.

When you have agreed your future possibilities, you then need to consider the half-way point from now to there and back again. These lists of 'intents' and plans will be what you and your senior team really believe you can achieve in the timeframe, barring really major changes in the way we deliver education. Neither of the above lists should be longer than two sides of A4.

The final stage of the planning process is to consider all the developments, changes and standards you wish to achieve or maintain over the next one to three years. The key headings are then used by all the staff and budget holders to draw up the likely targets that could be achieved. The senior team then refine them to a working chart of priorities, responsibilities, timeframe, costs linked to budgets and responsibilities. Targets should be drawn up bearing the usual constraints in mind (that is they should be SMART – specific, measurable, achievable, relevant and timed).

Motivating staff

Before attempting to write your first or next plan you must make sure that the staff are with you, that they understand the key aspects of the school's vision and that they are keen to make things better, or keen to maintain them at a very high level. It is not possible to take all the people with you all of the time, but how much are you prepared to concede before saying no? Remember, it's a great life if you don't weaken!

The most important part of the job is, and will always be, the people. Treat them with dignity and respect at all times and show them that you value them. These standards should be maintained as much as possible. One failure here can take many months to recover. It really is all too easy to take staff for granted and however good our intentions at the start of the year, when things get tough we can forget the basic decencies. To help remember these it pays to have your PA write down every member of staff's birthday in your diary. It also pays to find out and write down the names of the partner of each member of staff and try to learn them. If you can show that you know some details about your staff it will pay enormous dividends in difficult times. Short five-line biographies can also help, but will be very time-consuming to prepare. Each is then read around the time of that member of staff's birthday.

Other strategies that help are occasional gifts and acts of generosity that go a long way. For example, Heads often provide cakes and tea in the staffroom at the end of term, some provide them every Friday. Others provide strawberries and cream in the summer. We have heard of one Head who holds a raffle in the staffroom each week with the first prize being that he will take one of the winning teacher's lessons the following week. The school funds there have, apparently, never been healthier!

Once again, small catchphrases learnt and used by all your senior team can ensure that staff are treated properly. One such, which applies equally to staff and to students, is 'public praise, private reprimand'. As a policy it can change the atmosphere at all levels in a school.

How you go about your job as Head has never been so important. The position is now a high profile, highly accountable job which requires all postholders to give a public account of their activities to a wide range of audiences. These audiences are not just your staff and students but also the parents, governors, local people and especially the local media. The possibility now of something local becoming something national or even global have never been greater. Education is in the public eye and is reputedly one of the three most important priorities of government today. This has two immediate effects, one which says be extra careful, 'I don't want to get anything wrong because it will be publicised widely'. The other which says 'This is an opportunity to manipulate politicians and those who hold the purse strings to maximise the potential benefits that could accrue to our school'. Providing you take care, the only way forward for a change leader is the second scenario. We have to be bold.

So, getting the tactics right concerns two major groups of people. One group is within your organisation, the other is all those sub-groups with whom you interact outside your organisation but to your benefit.

Internal tactics

Staff need to feel valued and making them part of the process of your strategy for the organisation is fundamental.

Creating the culture has been dealt with in Chapter 4; however, there is also a cultural approach to planning and strategy that is important to you personally as Head. Culture, as we have said, is about expectation, standards, style and way of life. Giving ownership of the planning process within the parameters of the vision depends on how you tackle issues and present solutions, deal with tough questions and take decisions. These are all integral parts of the process and are closely linked to your own personal style and way of learning.

For all of these you have to have facts and information to begin with, enough of them enable understanding which leads on to knowledge. Use of knowledge over time brings wisdom. You have to work at all of these all the time. All of this now enables you to make better decisions.

TASK 27

Gathering information

Go back to Task 23 and ensure you have identified your preferred learning style.

Having decided on your strongest and weakest methods, ensure that you have information and knowledge given to you in the most appropriate way as often as possible. When this is not so, be aware and take extra care to understand in these cases. If need be you could also try to put the information into its most useful format before you have to make a decision. You may wish to use this approach with those particularly difficult decisions.

Things get worse before they get better

Your plan is in place, you have given responsibilities to relevant staff, the mission and aims have been articulated, the governors have agreed the plans, finally you begin implementation. (A word of warning: make sure that you have a second strategy available if the first one does not seem to be working. Be sure that you have been through all the 'if then' scenarios and you have a counter ready for each negative outcome.) Two months later things are in a mess. Everyone has started bickering, morale is low, no one seems to understand and the staff seem to be working in opposite directions.

Don't panic!

Change always brings a downturn after the initial euphoria and it will take time for its positive effect to work through. This is where your leadership is absolutely critical. You have to have faith in the change and know how to see it through. Make sure that you are monitoring closely and that you know how to recognise milestones and potholes. Use some of your alternative strategies to get round problems. Do some green and yellow hat thinking with the key staff, definitely *no* black hat thinking. Hold tight and give encouragement where necessary and personal support wherever you can. Monitor closely, measure constantly but quietly, and praise success loudly as soon as you find it.

If the change does not respond to treatment and tender loving care then you will need to look very carefully at the causes and see if you can eliminate them. If this does not work there may be a flaw in your logic from the initial solution to the action plan. Unless you have made a serious mistake then it is likely that the problems will be overcome.

If nothing works to overcome the problem and disillusionment turns to resentment you may have to abandon the change. If you do have to, do it with good grace and swiftly and then analyse carefully why it did not work. The learning will be very significant even though your ego may be badly bruised.

Summary

Our intention is that, at the end of this chapter, you will have:

- learnt that planning is crucial to change, and that better planning leads to smoother change

- learnt to write a detailed five-year development plan

- understood that a plan is only a set of guides and targets and that changes during a cycle may demand changes to the plan, which should be kept under constant review

- gained some of the skills needed to keep staff motivated and to maintain high morale
- analysed your own personal style and used the knowledge to develop strategies for staff management
- realised that change always leads to lowering of morale and standards in its early stages and that steps need to be taken to minimise this effect
- recognised the need for patience when implementing change.

chapter eight

Quality: monitoring, inspection and self review

Introduction

All schools now seek to be improving schools or to maintain the high standards they have already reached. The interesting thing about quality is that it is hard to measure, is somewhat subjective but we know it when we find it. However, we also know that it never happens accidentally. As John Ruskin put it:

> 'Quality is never an accident, it is always the result of intelligent effort.'

Monitoring

What do we measure and collect data on in order to ensure that we are maintaining and improving the standards in the schools we run? The simple strategy of regular observations of classroom practice is now commonplace. So too are the criteria by which we can judge a good lesson; the Ofsted criteria may not be everyone's favourite but they do form a consistent set of standards by which to judge teaching and learning in a traditional educational setting.

TASK 28

Criteria for quality

What additional criteria would you use to judge the quality of teaching and learning in an ICT rich learning environment? Reference to Chapter 10 might be of some assistance.

As with all that we do we can monitor in three places to assess the effect of the process:

- we can monitor the inputs (teaching)
- we can monitor the process itself (classroom activity)

- we can monitor the outputs (examination results, drama productions, sports results, artwork, percentage of students in jobs and so on).

Apart from classroom observation, what other activities and processes (normally called performance indicators) should we monitor in our schools:

- examination results
- student behaviour
- exclusions
- attendance
- vandalism
- accidents
- visitors
- governors visiting
- industry/business links
- new developments
- finances
- maintenance
- staff attendance
- percentage of lessons lost
- staff training
- school roll
- visits away from the school
- library use
- new technology use
- school development plans?

TASK 29

Performance indicators

For each of these aspects of school life try to find performance indicators that can be objectively measured and reported in numerical form. Decide which are inputs, processes and outputs. How frequently should each be measured?

Draw up a chart to record the data similar to Table 8.1 below.

TABLE 8.1 Performance indicators			
Performance indicator	**Current period**	**Previous period**	**Same period last year**
Lesson observation			
% outstanding and good			
% satisfactory			
% unsatisfactory			
Student attendance			
% attendance in Y7			
% attendance in Y8			
Reasons for student absence			
Medical			
Holidays			
Other			
GCSE examination results			
% five A* – C			
% five A* – G			
% one A* – G			
And so on …			

Having done this and recorded some results for your own school, the next task is to ask two colleague Heads to do the same with their schools. One should be similar in background, intake and achievement and the other should be one of the best performing schools of a similar type and size. You then have a set of standards to compare yourself to and also a set of standards to aspire to. If you are Head of a specialist school then the Technology Colleges Trust is likely to have significant amounts of data with which you can compare your performance.

Then there is your PandA data as another set of information that can be used in a variety of ways to compare your performance to national standards in a range of different ways, free school meals not withstanding. PandA documents explain clearly the basis on which the grades are given and the way in which the standards are obtained, so there is no need to repeat them here. It may, however, be of value to compare your PandA information with the two schools whose performance indicators you have already compared to your own.

Inspections

One of the first statements produced by an early Total Quality Management (TQM) business in this country that sticks in the mind when the word Ofsted is mentioned is:

> 'You can't inspect quality into a system.'

There has always seemed something of a dilemma about the Ofsted process as a result. Nonetheless it seems fair to say that the Ofsted process has sharpened up every aspect of the educational process in England, although there are many who would say the price has been very high. In hindsight we don't think there is a dilemma between the TQM statement and the Ofsted process since the inspection process has not been about trying to inspect quality into the system so much as to show each school its position in relation to other schools.

However, when we get to grips with the process and leave the horror stories and the bad publicity behind, those schools which have been quick to understand what is happening have used the inspection process to develop their own monitoring systems and build up effective self-evaluation systems which are at least as rigorous as the Ofsted process.

Whatever we may think of Ofsted inspections, they have made schools much more aware of why they are in business. The schedule for inspections published in January 2000 identifies two types of inspection, full and short. The Handbook appears a much more refined document, concentrating as ever on the quality of teaching and learning in the classroom and on the efficiency and effectiveness of the education provided. It appears much more sensitive to the many different types of school and the wide variety of intakes and social situations schools find themselves in. The toughness is still there and no excuses are allowed for failure to improve over time. As a Head, this approach provides support and encouragement to the strong demands that can be made to ensure that standards and the monitoring of them are not allowed to be watered down. Make use of these standards to set and maintain your own as you seek to improve the school that you lead.

This new, more flexible approach suggests that the process has now gone through its developmental stage and has reached the developed or mature stage.

Preparing for an inspection is still traumatic, since the results are published on the web and all your strengths and weaknesses as a school are there to be seen and pored over by the whole world. Getting it right with a six-week preparation time is still a challenge. The single most effective way of minimising the tension is to ensure that most, if not all, the inspection processes are part of the normal monitoring processes that have become endemic to the life and culture of the school. The inspection should then be very much an opportunity to celebrate the achievements of the school as much as anything else.

TASK 30

Linking school monitoring to the Ofsted process

As if we need to say it, study the latest Ofsted Handbook for Inspecting Schools in your phase and make yourself familiar with every aspect of it. Make sure your senior colleagues are also familiar with it.

Draw up a table similar to Table 8.2 below containing all of the inspection processes and next to each list the process that you use in your school to monitor that function. Any gaps will require new monitoring or management processes to be introduced, if you think it is necessary to do so.

TABLE 8.2 Ofsted and school monitoring processes

Ofsted process	School process
Lesson observations using standard proforma	Lesson observations by line managers and senior staff using Ofsted pro forma.
Check overall improvements since last report	Action plan regularly reviewed at all school meetings and in SDP. Changes recorded.

List all the documents and policies that any good school would have and which might be needed before or during an inspection. Allocate the preparation and updating of all these documents and policies among the staff.

Preparing for Ofsted inspection

If you are about to have a visit from the inspection team then follow the advice given by the professional associations, such as the Secondary Heads Association (SHA) or National Association of Head Teachers. They have accumulated evidence from all their members over the past seven years and have a wealth of experience. We could not hope to better their advice and we strongly recommend that you read their publications and attend one of their short training seminars as soon as that brown envelope has been opened.

The key to the inspection being a trouble-free experience is your own professionalism and that of the registered inspector. As soon as possible make contact with him or her and explain what you and your school wish to gain from the inspection, how you are going to manage the week and find out what the inspection team's priorities are. The SHA text includes full lists of documents required and includes a few suggestions about managing the inspection that are worth repeating here.

1 Ensure that every member of staff makes three copies of all their lesson plans before the week starts. Then, if observed, the inspector receives one copy and you another.

2 Use an interview proforma for staff to record all interactions with inspectors and submit these to you at the end of each day. By 5.00 pm you will then have a clear picture of what has been happening and how the staff have coped. If there are any comments that suggest that a member of staff has become upset through their meeting with an inspector you can contact that staff member that evening and reassure them. A senior member of staff can always visit the individual if necessary.

You will have found out the key themes that the inspection team has been following and the issues they are still trying to understand. You and the senior team can then prepare additional information for that early morning meeting with the registered inspector. As Head, you need to stay in control of the inspection, if you do not you will suffer a very strange sensation, that of being responsible for the school but not in control of it!

_____ Self review and the learning school _____

As standards are raised, the way quality is measured changes. Instead of it being external – by someone else measuring the school and the individual – the process becomes internalised. Quality becomes part of the culture.

How do you know when you have achieved this?

The self review or self audit process are used. One of the most effective available is that published by the Technology Colleges Trust, _Standards Audit_. It works by collecting all the data that can be compared to other schools and internally doing the comparison: examination and test results overall, and subject by subject, attendance data, destinations data, staying on rates and so on.

Then there are a set of criteria for a range of qualitative measures that are self-assessed against four classifications. These are basic, developing, developed and extended. Each department and cost centre carries out the audit and can draw up a table to summarise the information.

TABLE 8.3 Self review standards audit

Audit area	Basic	Developing	Developed	Extended
Standards				
Students' response				
Teaching				
Knowledge and skill				
Teacher expectations				
Planning				
Assessment				
Homework				
Partnerships with parents and community				
Monitoring				
Learning environment				

For each area there are indicative criteria which help the department to decide which level they have reached. The process is best carried out on a training day, but will require time before and after to complete the audit.

After this has been done once it should become a regular process in the school, with new areas and revised indicative criteria of your own being introduced. Departments should then moderate one another. You may also wish to invite in external professionals or another Head to assist in the moderation of the review. When you have reached this stage then you will certainly have reached the extended level in the area of self review!

The other process that reaches 'extended' standard with the right learning culture in the school, is learning itself. The school then becomes a 'learning school'. Indicative criteria for this might include those listed in Table 8.4.

TABLE 8.4 Indicative criteria of a learning school

- Investors In People Standard obtained for more than four years

- Charter Mark may also have been obtained

- Staff regularly work on educational research

- Many staff have gained, or are in the process of gaining, higher degrees

- The school is likely to be part of a teacher training scheme (SCITT)

- The school may be a Beacon School

- Staff regularly provide training for other teachers, schools and local businesses.

TASK 31

Indicative criteria

Based on the areas identified in Table 8.3 above, draw up three indicative criteria for each of the grades of Basic, Developing, Developed and Extended for each area. When you have completed this, check your criteria against those published in the Standards Audit (available from the Technology Colleges Trust, 23rd Floor, Millbank Tower, Millbank, London SW1P 4QP, www.tctrust.net).

———— Summary ————

Our intention is that, at the end of this chapter, you will have:

- recognised that regular monitoring is essential to success

- established benchmarks by which to judge your school now and in five years' time

- appreciated the role of Performance Indicators in raising standards

- devised a process to make the whole school focus on improvements in teaching and learning, and effectiveness and efficiency

- gained confidence in your ability to achieve results and to be aware of your standards

- developed a plan to introduce self-review – an effective tool to make quality part of your culture.

chapter nine

Leadership in action

Introduction

Some of the key features of leadership have been outlined in Chapter 2. This chapter presents some exercises designed to develop your leadership skills and then looks at leadership styles. It will end with study of the characteristics of effective school leaders.

Leadership skills

The function of the school leader is so important that we think it merits further attention. After all Hay Mcber found in their research on effective Heads that 70 per cent of the success (or failure) of a school was directly attributable to the Head. We have an enormous responsibility to carry. Proper preparation for leadership is essential, as is the refining and honing of the skill once we have become Heads.

The NPQH list of leadership skills states that:

> *Headteachers should be able to use appropriate leadership styles in different situations in order to:*
>
> *i.   create and secure commitment to a clear vision for an effective institution;*
>
> *ii   initiate and manage change and improvement in pursuit of strategic objectives;*
>
> *iii prioritise, plan and organise;*
>
> *iv   direct and co-ordinate the work of others;*
>
> *v   build, support and work with high performing teams;*
>
> *vi   work as part of team;*
>
> *vii devolve responsibilities, delegate tasks and monitor practice to see that they are being carried out;*
>
> *viii motivate and inspire pupils, staff, parents, governors and the wider community*
>
> *ix   set standards and provide a role model for staff;*

> x   seek advice and support when necessary;
>
> xi   deal sensitively with people and resolve conflicts.
>
> Headteachers should have the professional competence and expertise to:
>
> xii   command credibility through the discharge of their functions and to influence others;
>
> xiii   provide professional direction to the work of others;
>
> xiv   make informed use of inspection and research findings;
>
> xv   apply good practice from other sectors and organisations.

The 'X' factor

A list like that provides you with a tick list but it leaves something out. It doesn't tell you how to develop those elusive qualities – presence, charisma, style – that create your personality as a Head and enable other people to be inspired by your leadership. We can only say that they are personal to you and to each Head. The Hay Mcber research seems to suggest there are as many different ways of putting together the essential qualities of a Head with her or his personal characteristics, as there are Heads. This implies that although there are some standard functions that all successful people do, there is an 'X' factor that cannot be bottled and which is unique to each Head. From discussions with other Heads of schools that are seeking to challenge norms and wishing to take risks, these successful leaders are always aware of themselves and how they relate to their communities in ways that you don't find elsewhere. To use Howard Gardner's multiple intelligences concept, Heads appear to have high intra-personal and interpersonal intelligences. What follows in this chapter attempts to provide ways of improving them.

MBWA

TASK 32

MBWA with staff

We introduced the concept of management by walking about (MBWA) in Chapter 2. The task here is to write down three questions that you would like to ask each member of staff in order to get to know them better as professional colleagues; staff here means all employees of the school.

Over the next half-term make a point of speaking to as many staff as possible to ask them one or more of the questions. Intersperse it among your normal conversations. Some possible questions:

- What has gone really well this week? Can you explain why?
- What has gone badly this week? Why?
- What do like about the school? Why?
- What do you dislike about the school? Why?
- Who's doing well/badly in your classes at the moment?
- What would you like to change about the school if you had the chance?
- What are the main frustrations about the job and what could we do to reduce them?

Observe areas where people work, comment as necessary, both positively as well as negatively. Keep in mind the 80/20 principle; four positive comments need to be made for every negative one. Invite constructive comment, always challenge negative thinking. Questions should seek to find information about your performance indicators, but in a qualitative manner. Remember also the rule of three: if you hear information about anything or anyone from three or more sources over a short period of time it is imperative that some action is taken, whether it be praise, analysis or reprimand.

TASK 33

MBWA with students

In a similar way to the previous task, identify a range of questions to ask students and then spend time on a regular basis at break and lunchtime, before school and after school talking to them. Mix your three key questions with your normal conversations with students about sport, current music and films, etc.

- What subject/lesson do you enjoy most at the moment? Why?
- What subject do you enjoy least at the moment? Why?
- What do you like/hate most about school? Why?
- What would you most like to change about school if you could? Why?
- Are you able to cope with all your work at present? What could be done to help?
- Have you been on any visits/trips recently? Did you enjoy them?

■ What do you do after school? Do you play for any school teams, take part in clubs?

There are many more questions that can be asked and we invite you to design some more of your own that suit you own environment. Again, remember to take action if the same kind of comment comes up more than three times in a short space of time.

When doing these regular tours, daily if you can and certainly every day in your first year of headship, keep an eye out for damage, tidiness, litter and graffiti. Changes in these are very powerful signs as to whether the school is improving or getting worse. They can never be ignored.

TASK 34

MBWA with parents

The ability to talk directly with parents is very difficult at a secondary school because there is not the collection of parents waiting at the gate as there is in primary schools. The use of letters home with comment sections for return, or annual questionnaires can be very valuable as they provide benchmarks for you to monitor if some of the same questions are asked each year. A good way to start is to use the pre-inspection Ofsted Questionnaire. It is fairly general but it makes a good basis from which to add one or two of your own questions each year about current relevant topics.

Analyse the results and take action on immediate issues, both individual concerns and whole school wherever you can. The bigger and more time-consuming and, therefore, costly issues will probably have to wait and be incorporated into future plans.

It is more difficult to read the signs by direct personal contact beyond the school but it is important to maintain good communication with other groups within your community. Generally your governing body will hear most of the feedback as they will represent many of the local groups and be in regular contact with many more.

Data collection

The above activities should help keep you in touch with qualitative information, which is subjective and not always reliable. It deals with feelings and perceptions rather than hard facts. It is increasingly important to listen to the feelings and to understand perceptions but it is also vital to have the hard data as well. Identifying the important hard data about your school that you collect regularly is vital if the qualitative information is to be balanced. So the next task is a refresher!

TASK 35

Hard data collection

With your senior team draw up a list of all the factual data you could collect about your school and its activities – quantitative performance indicators. Only reject what is too time consuming to collect easily (wasted effort is one of the most frustrating aspects of the job). Place these items in priority in a chart like the one below and then rigorously implement it. Publish the information widely in the school and regularly discuss it with your senior team.

TABLE 9.1 Quantitative performance indicators

Performance indicator	Data	Frequency of collection	Responsibility
Student attendance	%	weekly	Miss Smith
Reasons for absence		weekly	
Medical	%		
Holiday	%		
Personal	%		
Damage	Cost	monthly	
Staff absence		monthly	
Medical	%		
Training	%		
Personal	%		
Public examination		Every year	
Results			

This gives some idea of how to start. Limit the regular report to no more than two sides of A4 otherwise there will be too much data to analyse, and too much information can be as useless as too little. Refer back to the information in Chapter 8 about performance indicators if you need to.

———— Taking risks ————

Leadership is not about being foolhardy but it does involve risk. Consider the number of Heads of Fresh Start schools that have left within the first year of their tenure. (Fresh Start is a programme of rebadging existing schools that have failed by renaming them and bringing in a new Head and senior staff. The Heads have all been appointed from existing posts in successful schools.) It is the Head's duty to minimise risk since each child in her or his care has one chance in the school and so it is fundamental to all that we do maximise the chances of success for each student.

But to be successful in improving our schools we have to become change leaders which will necessarily involve risk. The dilemma is never fully resolved, all we can do is act to minimise that risk. The message we are receiving today is that by retaining the status quo we are taking more risk with our students' futures than if we embrace change.

Risk can be minimised by:

- careful and thorough planning
- carrying out risk assessments
- building a network of like-minded colleagues and contacts
- having a clear vision of where you are going and how you are going to get there
- having a strong and supportive personal life
- having very good monitoring systems
- creating a continuous improvement culture and a positive atmosphere
- having good contingency plans
- understanding new technology
- having a passion for excellence
- being relentless in pursuit of your goals
- being a good communicator.

———— Communication ————

Presenting information is one of the most important attributes of a Head. The range of audience you have to speak to is vast and the numbers are often large as well. So how you communicate with each constituency is vital for your leadership. Also very important is the frequency of communication with each constituency, nobody likes to feel ignored even if you are very busy.

New technology is making new ways of communication, many of them simpler and faster than existing ones. This, paradoxically, makes our job of managing our communications more difficult – there are more to choose from and how do you decide which is now best? Many schools now have web pages and some allow interaction between home and school directly on them by e-mail or other link.

The methods available are changing all the time, but this is one of those personal areas that help you to define yourself as a Head to your community. You have to choose the most suitable way to tell people about events, children's progress and the school's progress. Remember that most people in your community can only have about five minutes of your time a year; they know you through your publications:

- assemblies

- prospectus

- letters home

- newsletters

- annual report

- newspaper articles about the school

- local radio interviews

- questionnaires

- meetings where you speak from a platform

- events

- web site

- e-mail

- electronic discussion forums.

For each one you have to have a style and a strategy for conveying any message. Experience suggests that however carefully you plan, some people will always misunderstand the message. The above list is just a starting point and we invite you to find other ways in which you might wish to communicate with your outside community.

The staff, however, see and speak to you most and your communication with them is even more important. They have to be encouraged, cajoled and motivated to give of their best for the school. They will normally give of their best for the students because that is why they came into education. Chapter 11 considers these issues in more detail.

———— Leadership styles ————

Leadership styles are, according to Hay Mcber, the way in which the leader:

- listens
- sets goals and standards
- develops action plans
- directs others
- gives feedback.

The six styles that were identified by the Hay Group when they conducted their research into effective heads are:

- coercive
- authoritative
- affiliative
- democratic
- pacesetting
- coaching.

They found that there is no one best style and effective leadership is using the appropriate style with specific people in specific situations. They go on to say that leadership styles are a function of:

- your personal characteristics (personality, values, principles)
- styles you have seen and experienced others using
- the school's espoused values as to the right way to manage
- the specific management situation and the people you deal with most.

The research also identifies six key areas that are critical for school improvement and that are strongly influenced by the leadership styles used in the school:

- flexibility
- responsibility
- standards
- rewards
- clarity
- team commitment.

From their analysis they find that the best Heads and deputies:

- focus on data, quality of teaching and learning, referring to standards and targets to raise achievement
- are outcome oriented and *measure* progress through results and monitoring
- have *huge* amounts of energy and commitment to step change in performance and are relentless in their focus on raising standards
- are driven by a core set of values which underpin their vision
- share leadership, involve others, ask for help, and are outward-focused.

They also found that:

- the very best new Heads are doing as well as the best established Heads
- the best deputy headteachers contribute significantly to the school's performance.

They also found that successful Heads

> 'act quickly to tackle under-performance, take a strategic view aimed at transforming performance and create time and space to take risks'.

FIG. 9.1 Model of Leadership Effectiveness

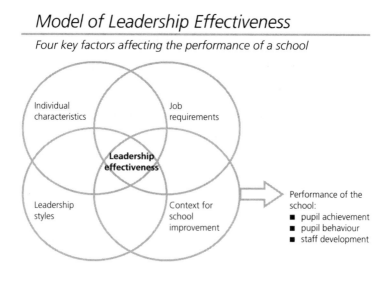

Model of Leadership Effectiveness
Four key factors affecting the performance of a school

Taken from the research by Hay Mcber and used in the LPSH programme.

———— Summary ————

Our intention is that, at the end of this chapter, you will have:

- developed the use of management by walking about (MBWA) in a systematic and thorough manner so that it has become a vital leadership tool in collecting qualitative data for regularly interacting with your staff and students

- learnt to acquire quantitative data regularly as essential hard evidence, chosen from appropriate performance indicators, to inform planning and decision-making

- created a risk-tolerant culture that is essential for sustained school improvement

- understood your own leadership styles and used them effectively, balancing tasks with styles as appropriate

- applied time management techniques to create the time and space to take risks.

chapter ten

The power of technology

Introduction

This chapter explains technological thinking and its importance to the role of the change leader in deciding what really matters. It then goes on to suggest ways of making the best use of the information in IT or ICT as it relates to the job of Head. The chapter closes with a brief speculation on how the interaction of technology with the school leader might develop in the next ten years.

The need for passion

To be a head teacher and a change leader in the 21st century we would argue that a certain passion for new technology is essential. We live in a society that relies on science and technology for its wellbeing and on technology for all the links between us. We don't mean a passion for the technology itself but a passion for and an understanding of what technology can do for our organisations and communities. The complete text of this book from start to finish has been in digital format, only two pages of hand written comments and sketches have ever been produced. Twenty years ago this would have been virtually impossible. In 20 years' time what new ways of storing information and communication will have been developed?

For example, how would you like your students to learn about the battle of Marathon:

- listen to a teacher talking about the battle
- read from a text book in English
- read from a text in classical Greek
- read from a text with pictures – hand drawn – to try to convey something of the image of the scene beyond the words
- watch a filmed reconstruction of the battle and discuss with an historian.

- read from a text on a disk or CD-ROM with links to other references

- read about it from a text on the Internet with links to whatever references are available

- read from an interactive text on the Internet where it is possible to enter a chat room with experts and ask any questions about Greece in 490BC that you wish to.

- enter a multimedia world where the student can become one of the participants in the battle in a simulated/film version in whichever language best suits the student. Then the student can link by netcam to an historian to discuss the tactics used in the battle.

- travel back in time to witness the actual event accompanied by an historian, observe the battle and discuss with the historian all the questions that the student can possibly think up about the Greeks and the Persians?

All but the last scenario can be ways to learn about this event in history. The penultimate is perhaps not really available today, although we do have the technology to create it, but do we want to and for whom does it have value?

The last scenario is given because it is unreal and inconceivable at the present time because of our understanding gained from current scientific knowledge, but perhaps we should not ignore the possibility in the future.

There are two important issues here which we think that Heads have to confront.

1 Scientists and technologists seem capable of turning ideas into reality at an ever increasing pace. We as leaders in our communities have to have views on the validity of the machines being developed, their influence on our society and the way in which we should use them or allow them to be used. The challenge to our moral and ethical values grows with each new advance in science and engineering. This is particularly so in the fields of medicine and computers. We think that Heads have to have clear views on these matters in order to give leadership to their communities within and without the school.

2 The last example given as a way of learning about the Battle of Marathon is so obviously impossible that we dismiss it immediately. Nonetheless there is that slight doubt at the back of one's mind that says, however faintly, 'not yet possible, but maybe some day'. The history of the human species is such that we have to be extremely careful about saying 'it will never happen'. Just think of the 'advances', or perhaps we should say changes, over the past 200 years. No one alive in 1800 could possibly imagine most of our normal everyday lives today. What will be possible in 2200?

Be aware of tomorrow's technology

As a Head of a school it is not necessary, yet, to be prescient, but it is necessary to be aware of some of the changes that are likely to come along in the next five years. How is this possible? For example, the British Telecom website contains the company's internal magazine that is available to all visitors to the site. Once a year they publish an edition that considers the likely technology changes over the next few years. As they say on the site, the items listed to come to market in the next three years are already at the prototype stage or have been demonstrated experimentally in the laboratory. They are being developed and if there is a market for them they will become available in the shops. The authors then speculate on the likely impact of these devices. We as Heads need to speculate on their likely impact on education and how much notice we should take.

If we think a machine will be beneficial then we should speed up the process by contacting the site at the address given. Likewise we should slow down the process if we think the device is detrimental.

As we said earlier change leaders have to *make* the future not respond to it. That old prayer which is still regularly used in our assemblies seems even more poignant now:

> God, grant me the courage to change the things I can,
> grant me the serenity to accept the things I cannot
> and grant me the wisdom to know the difference.

Technology is changing our world; let us make use of it to make a better one. We must make technology the servant and not the master. To do this we have to know as much as possible about it.

Technological thinking

Technology can be very simple. It has become complicated because it means so many things to different people. To some it is the old craft subjects repackaged, to others it is computers and to others it is another name for engineering. To all of these it is also a process, that is a way of tackling problems. The technological process is used mostly in the three areas above, and is the most effective way of acquiring the skills and knowledge inherent in those subjects. From the Head's point of view the area of interest should be new technological devices, of which computers are only one, and how these are likely to affect the way we think and work.

How computers work

All digital systems work by electrical switches that are either on or off. They are, therefore, called binary devices because they use binary codes to work. All computers and all machines that have microprocessors or chips all work in exactly the same way at a fundamental level. They are entirely logical and are based on the algebraic relationships that exist between these strings of digits. All inputs, processing and outputs are managed by the computer or machine in this same way, either the signal is 'on' or it is 'off'. So it is always true that if you put garbage in you will always get garbage out.

So what? Well, the consequence is that all processing by machine is carried out in exactly the same way, which means that you as the leader of the organisation knows how each machine 'thinks'. This then enables you to work with the machines and with the people who use them because it is a simple process to predict behaviour.

The fascinating idea behind computers is that almost all behaviour can be reduced to a series of '0's' and '1's'. The mathematics behind digital processing is called boolean algebra and develops what we would call computer logic. By developing truth tables for mixtures of logic gates (on/off switches) it is soon possible to understand the rudiments of the microprocessor. Although not essential for a Head, a basic understanding of boolean algebra will not go amiss.

TASK 36

Logic gates

Find out about the following logic gates and write truth tables for them.

- AND

- NOT

- OR

- NAND

- NOR

If you have used the advanced searches on an Internet search engine, such as Yahoo!, you will have noticed that they include the logic statements AND and OR in these searches.

You cannot afford to be a technophobe

As computer scientists gain ever more understanding of how the brain works and how we react to situations, the easier it becomes to digitise human behaviour. As our capability to build ever more complex machines grows, so does our capacity to translate human endeavour to machine. For example, even the best chess player in the world can now only sometimes beat the best chess machine in the world. Soon machines will be able to think as quickly as people and as intuitively. Thus the capacity to build an electronic teacher or robot is getting closer. It is, however, unlikely that such a machine will be in existence for another 20 years, but the projection is included to give you some clue as to where computing technology is going. Soon all courses will be available for study at home, soon it will be possible to contact a tutor for support across the web at any time of the day or night. There are already examples of this happening. The list of projections, scare stories or fantasies could go on. As a Head it is necessary to take a view on the power of technology and how much of an impact it can or should make on the school.

It is imperative that the knowledge of computers and scientific and technological thought processes is much better than simply a nodding acquaintance with the subject. Not that any Head has to be a 'nerd', but it is vital that you cannot be hoodwinked or deceived by the IT, science or technology staff within the organisation. Remember each person has his or her own agenda.

CASE STUDY

A few years ago there was a school which regarded itself as a sound exemplar of the use of technology. The Head was a graduate in History and the senior team consisted of former heads of science, business studies, art and modern languages. They had been able to do many things with the IT network that existed. However, quite often when they asked for the system to perform some new function for the school, they would be told that it was not possible, either on their system or any other computer system. The response would sometimes happen in a more roundabout way from the information systems manager: 'We will try and see if it will work. It might be possible, but I am not sure that there is any technology that is capable of that at present.' A week or two later the response would come back: 'Sorry, but it's not possible; we have tried but it just can't be done yet.' Somehow even when other people were called in to help they would end up agreeing with the IS manager.

Then a new member of staff with a background in IT joined the senior team. When requests were made for the system to do as required, the usual response came back. After a few months the new senior member of staff sent a note to the IS manager as follows: 'I have been most disappointed with the performance of the network since I arrived and your department's responses to my concerns. I propose to call in an IT professional after the holiday to examine the performance of the network and suggest improvements. Do you have any comments before I proceed?'

The reply came back: 'I resign.'

The IS manager left soon afterwards and has been able to succeed in a job more suited to his talents. The school has been able to go from strength to strength, but that person had held up the development of IT in that school for more than five years. No one had the vision of what technology could achieve, the knowledge to back up that vision, nor the leadership to drive through the change. Worst of all, the school had not understood that it had the wrong person in this important post.

The message here is that unless there is a strong vision and very considerable knowledge within the senior team or ready access to it outside that can be trusted, then it is necessary for the Head to have a considerable knowledge of the capability and the limitations of the new technology.

Our education system over the past 50 years, whether public or private, appears to have been doing its best to prevent students becoming well-rounded adults in terms of knowledge. It has, as C. P. Snow put it, developed adults who live in one of 'two cultures'. For example, it is not uncommon to hear a supposedly, well-educated person saying, almost proudly: 'I was no good at science at school so I gave it up in the third form.' You would never hear anyone proudly admitting that they were no good at Shakespeare and so gave up studying his work in the third form. The example is somewhat exaggerated, but nonetheless makes a point that still rings true. If there is one very clear message that access to so much information gives us it is that if we want to turn this information into knowledge, understanding and wisdom, then we all have to become 'Renaissance men and women'.

As change leaders we cannot allow any lack of scientific and technological understanding to hold us back and we cannot rely entirely on others. We have to have some understanding of this thinking and the digital revolution to maximise its use for good in our communities.

TASK 37

Philosophy of science

Read the following classic texts on the philosophy of science, if you are not already familiar with them. They help a great deal in understanding how science (and then technology) influences the way our world thinks and acts, without becoming too technical.

The Logic of Scientific Discovery   Karl R. Popper

The Structure of Scientific Revolutions   Thomas S. Kuhn

Write a review of the two books in about 200 words for each one.

Making best use of technology: fitting it to the vision

With the rate of change of technology so fast and life spans of technological equipment being so short, it is impossible to be specific about any individual technology. What this section attempts to make clear is that a set of guidelines can be drawn up which help to make decisions about technology easier and more reliable for the non-expert. Certainly the Secondary Heads Association has published a very good booklet about the role of ICT in school and we suggest that this should be consulted as well.

TASK 38

Developing ICT policy

Take the vision of education that you have developed earlier or the one known and followed in the school in which you work, then consider the following questions.

1 What role, if any, does new technology play in the school at present?

2 What role does new technology play in students' and their parents' everyday lives?

3 How, ideally, should new technology be used for administration?

4 How, ideally, should new technology be used for management?

5 How, ideally, should new technology be used for leadership?

6 How, ideally, should it be used for teaching?

7 How for learning?

8 How for homework?

9 How for communication?

10 How for preparation for adult life?

The answers to these questions form the outline of the school's ICT policy.

It next makes sense to ask the logical and even more fundamental question as a corollary to the above: If we were starting to create a new school today, how would we use new technology from the foundations upwards? The answer to this question should flow from your vision of education that already exists. If it cannot then you haven't grasped the impact that new technology is going to make to all schools and it is necessary to revisit your vision. The phrase often used is reengineering, but redesigning is probably more appropriate. We remind you again of the quote by Andy Rosenfield who is part of the team that recently launched the first Internet university, Cardean University:

> 'The thing the Internet does least well is parrot the classroom, but we don't think this is the key part of education. The key part is making people do, think, interact, ask questions and form groups and the Internet is ideal for that.'
>
> (*The Times*, 1 July 2000)

Are you going to make sure that your school takes note of this comment? If so, how is it going to affect policy and practice within your organisation? Are there plans for students to interact with each other and with teachers over distances outside school hours? If not, why not – because you can be sure that the students are already doing this from their own homes, but the subject matter will not normally be school work.

What are we doing about this as educators? The greatest opportunity to transform educational culture, because this is exciting to all young people, is here, now with us. We have to be bold and grab it with both hands, otherwise what need will there be for normal school structures? If we return to what is said by Rosenfield – the Internet is ideal for the key parts of education – some more disturbing questions follow:

- Have you rethought the role of the school buildings in the 'school' of tomorrow?

- Have you rethought the role of the teacher in the school of tomorrow?

- What impact will wireless technology have on education?

- How soon will new forms of school develop?

- What preparations have you made for any of the possible changes?

But in order to be this bold the need to understand the power of the new technology is ever more demanding. Can you, as Head, rely on your information systems manager or your head of information and communications technology to come forward with the compelling argument and plans for the transformation of the teaching and learning culture?

The extract in Fig. 10.1 below is a page taken from the website, or better a group of electronic communities – human networks – being pioneered by Oracle. It can be found at the 'Think.com' website and allows a range of interaction between people in closed or open communities to study, discuss, question, share interests, in fact, do anything with information that any local, geographical community can do. In many ways it can do more because of the structure of the Internet and the site which are not so easy to replicate in geographical communities. The page displayed only shows the ways in which members can interact with each other.

It is shown because we need to pose the question of whether and how we should take note of such developments. If students are using this site to communicate with their teachers and experts around the world, we can surely use this to improve the quality of teaching and learning we offer to our students in their daily lives at school.

FIG. 10.1 Think.com's toolkit

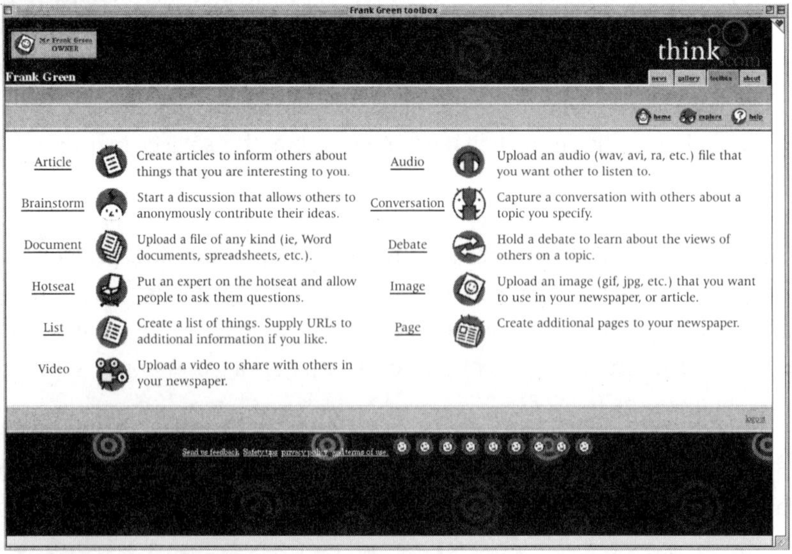

Networks

Very much an 'in' word today, technology has enabled us to communicate faster, more effectively and within our own control, with more people at a time, at a fraction of the cost of previous communication systems. At present it is in a much more uncontrolled way.

Current names for networks in use are shown in Table 10.1.

TABLE 10.1	Networks in use
LANs	Local Area Networks, such as the one you have in your school, generally relates to hardware.
WANs	Wide Area Networks, such as the one that links all the schools in the LEA or a group of schools within the LEA, generally relates to hardware.
Wireless Networks	Networks that are linked by radio signals similar in range to those used in mobile phones, normally in the 2.4GHz frequency. These can be local or wide area and are rapidly increasing in carrying capacity. This sector of the market is set to grow dramatically in the next few years. WAP (Wireless Application Protocol) phones are the first of the consumer devices available.
Intranet	Network linking a group of machines exclusively; no access to the outside world. The machines may be local or worldwide.
The Internet	Biggest of them all, anyone can join from anywhere with a few simple connections.

What these electronic networks are doing is creating new communities and new neighbourhoods which are no longer geographically based but exist worldwide. What account is your school taking of these changes in the very structure of society?

Moral issues and ethics

More disturbing is the ease with which young people today have access to information which in previous generations was only available to adults. This information includes pornography but extends to racist and violent material. It includes subversive technology and subversive ideas. Young people are gaining access to information which they think they understand but they do not have sufficient maturity to realise the full consequence of what they are doing.

This is having a major impact on our society. How are you planning to manage the debate in your school?

What action are you intending to take to provide the necessary moral and ethical leadership and education of your students in this area? Is what you do already sufficient?

None of this takes account of the advances that technology has allowed in science – especially genetics, medicine and micro-engineering.

Where does your school stand on the moral issues and questions raised by these advances?

Again, leadership has to be shown to our young people and if it doesn't come from the schools where is it going to come from?

Consequently knowing what products are likely to be available in the next few years seems to us to be an important part of the Head's role. Understanding how they might affect daily life and what moral or ethical questions might be raised by them is even more important it would seem. There are a number of publications that give information on the near future – products that are already at the pilot stage. One such is the BT Technology Journal which is available on the internet at bt.com/bttj.

Creativity in the digital age

One of the greatest effects that new technology is likely to have on the world is the development of human creativity. Many people have expressed their concern that the curriculum in schools is becoming too controlled and that there is not sufficient time for the more creative aspects of education. There have been many calls for a reduction in the content of the formal National Curriculum to allow more space for creative talent to be developed.

The power of technology is twofold. It can help to ensure that rigidity is built into the early years of formal education to ensure that mental discipline is encouraged. But because of its liberating potential when used creatively the technology has the capacity to encourage the human mind to think in far more imaginative ways. In the first instance the power of the computer can be programmed to force the user to follow specific sequences of learning and approaches to problem-solving. It is this very rigidity that helps train the mind when used with an effective teacher.

In the second instance, again, it is the capacity for repetitive work that helps to free the mind. The user no longer has to spend time on the dull parts of creative thinking or the time-consuming activities, the machine can be programmed to do these. The user is thus able to rely on the supportive role of the machine to allow the mind to wander and for the machine to provide assistance instantly when required. Moreover with neural and other networks enabling machines to become ever more 'intuitive' their capacity to help us think both logically and creatively is increasing day by day. Again the technology works best in the hands of a properly trained teacher, so we return once more to the need to train effective teachers for the 'Information Age'.

More teachers with more specialised skills is likely to be the long-term outcome of the full integration of new technology into education. However, if the system is too rigid, because it cannot adapt quickly enough to the changing demands of society, each parent could then become the effective teacher.

So we take the view that we need to find space to enable the new creative age to blossom whilst we ensure that there are enough proficient teachers to deliver this new curriculum.

———— Summary ————

Our intention is that, at the end of this chapter, you will have:

- seen that it is essential to embrace technology in education to improve schools

- recognised the need for leaders to understand scientific and technological thinking because we live in a scientific and technological world

- analysed and improved your own computing skills and interest in science and technology

- realised the importance of taking a view on current moral and ethical dilemmas posed by advances in science and technology

- understood that new communities and new networks are being created by technology to allow totally new ways of enthusing young people about learning

- realised that the Internet is changing the way we teach and learn and is likely to change the whole structure of schooling.

Leading and managing staff

Introduction

In the current climate it is difficult for teachers to feel secure since their role is changing so much and they have been pilloried so much in the press over recent times. Surveys indicate that most teachers actively seek to persuade their children not to enter the profession. However, almost all the teachers we know have always been very professional and very committed, even if we have disagreed about the best way to educate young people.

The guidelines to the NPQH programme state that –

> '*Effective headship results in:*
>
> *teachers who*
>
> - *have a secure knowledge and understanding of the subject(s) they teach;*
> - *set high expectations for pupils;*
> - *plan lessons which address the needs of all pupils within the class;*
> - *employ the most effective approach(es) for any given content and group of pupils;*
> - *pace lessons appropriately, using time and resources effectively;*
> - *regularly mark and assess pupils' work and reinforce and extend pupils' learning and achievement through setting consistent and challenging homework;*
> - *understand the importance of a regime of rules and discipline;*
> - *are systematically monitored, evaluated and supported in their work.'*

It is a tall order to achieve the above profiles for all your teachers. It is perhaps just an oversight, but we think that the word 'teachers' should be replaced by the word 'staff' in this statement since staff other than teachers are just as important to the school. This chapter aims to provide the new Head, or even the more experienced Head, with some pointers to keeping the staff motivated enough to come in willingly to work and to leave at the end of the day reasonably satisfied.

Assessing staff competencies

TASK 39

Staff competencies

As an initial exercise it would pay to assess your staff using the above criteria as a basis for developing competencies; it will give you some idea of the size of the task being faced. It may also be useful to use the characteristics identified in the Threshold Assessment process recently introduced.

To give some gradation to the assessments of each member of staff, each competence could be given a grade from 1 to 5. It would then be a useful exercise for the senior staff to carry out this assessment every year in order to build a picture of the kind of training in basic skills needed for the staff. It would also ensure that any support that was needed for staff could be prepared before the situation becomes critical. Being proactive is much less stressful than being reactive. This activity can be particularly relevant when there is a high turnover as happens in many schools in the South East of England and the inner cities. You might like to use a grid similar to the one given here.

TABLE 11.1 Staff competencies

Competence	Grade	Support needed
Knowledge and understanding		
Expectations		
Lesson planning		
Teaching		
Pupil progress		
Personal development		
Support for school policies		
Basic professional duties		

How do you know that each member of staff is competent to do the jobs they have been assigned to? In the previous chapter the situation in one school was explained where a member of staff without the necessary skills had been placed in a particularly difficult situation for him and where the school had suffered for a number of years. Unfortunately for that person he had been placed in such a position that he felt his only option was to leave. Maybe there was no alternative, but it is important that we at the top of the organisation retain the clarity of vision to see all the fine detail, especially when it is in matters relating to the staff. In that case the question that needs to be raised is: Did anyone on the senior team realise that the member of staff was out of his depth?

How frequently is a skills audit of the staff carried out? If it is not already an annual practice of value and substance, the new performance management procedures are going to make it essential. We believe it is important to make it a process that values existing skills and identifies training needs.

TASK 40

Performance management

Check that your performance management policy includes a skills audit. Design one in if it is not there, or highlight it if it does not stand out sufficiently. Ask the staff to design one rather than impose it.

Plan what you are going to do with the information once it has been gathered. It should form the basis for the staff training programme for the next year.

This skills audit is the basis for fair performance management. If the classroom teacher or laboratory assistant does not have the skills to do the job then we cannot criticise or blame them for their failure to carry out their job description to the required standard. If gaps in knowledge are identified then it is our responsibility to provide the necessary training.

Staff culture

Motivating the staff to want to walk through fire for you is the ideal goal. There are one or two Heads who have achieved this feat but it takes years of patience, nurturing, cajoling and sometimes even bullying to get there. Even adults, sometimes, have to be dragged kicking and screaming, metaphorically of course, into the culture that is being created. It also requires a steadfastness and trustworthiness that you have to develop, as well as a capacity to make each person you speak to or work with feel as if they are the most important person in the world.

It is essential to:

- show respect
- value each of them
- praise and reward when due
- reprimand and discipline when appropriate
- give your full attention to each
- know the fine details about each employee and remember them when necessary
- give each person space to do their job and not to interfere
- remove the fear of failure or blame culture
- not ask too much of anyone.

It is our observation, however, that teachers as a body have a great capacity to put themselves down and to see the glass as half empty as opposed to half full. All staffs whinge, whatever the organisation and however good the working conditions. Listen to concerns and learn to manage them. A sure sign of serious concern is when they start asking their representatives to meet you and they in turn start to remind you who they are. It will pay to listen carefully at an early stage. If you are having to manage a difficult issue it will help to be proactive and speak to staff representatives before taking any action. This is so that they understand the issues from the school's perspective first before they hear a half-baked story from someone who has overheard two snippets of conversation and made two and two come to seven. Chinese whispers is still a great game and everyone loves a bit of scandal.

One principle we would recommend when dealing with staff and students is 'public praise, private reprimand'. It helps build trust and confidence. There is no situation that we have come across where public humiliation of staff has any positive benefits. In fact, it invariably makes matters worse. The reason is obvious: it destroys self esteem and the dignity of the individual. Ruling by fear may have been appropriate in the past but it has no place in 21st century organisations. Other ways of speaking to staff that you should avoid are:

- repeated public nagging at staff as a whole
- public condemnation of an action by a member of staff to the staff as a whole, even though the individual is not mentioned
- public sarcasm in relation to an individual.

We have taken a strongly supportive role of junior members of staff because they have to be valued most, since it is they who deliver the educational service every day to children, their parents and the outside world. Whether it is in the classroom or on the telephone or at reception, these people are the face of the school and ensuring that they are valued and respected in a genuine way is crucial to the long-term success of the organisation. Viewed from a financial perspective, it is essential to remember that staffing costs in schools absorb about 75% of the available funds. It therefore makes a great deal of sense to ensure that staff welfare is properly taken care of and, since time means money, spending the necessary time with them.

Set clear guidelines

All people like to work within guidelines because having some certainties gives people the confidence to take risks in other areas. So it is also important to set clear ground rules as to the standards expected of staff that reflect the image of the school to its best effect. Whether teachers like it or not, they are role models for young people and sometimes the only supportive adult they meet in their daily lives. As the commercial says 'No one forgets a good teacher'.

So despite the support and encouragement that you give the staff, it is important that there are clear lines of authority and communication. They need to know that there are some items that are not negotiable, leaders are paid to lead and managers are paid to manage. Staff need to understand the difference between direction, consultation and democracy. They also need to know when each is in operation.

Staff as knowledge workers

The skills that teachers have are increasingly the same as those required of knowledge workers in other sectors of the economy. As we enter the knowledge society of the 21st century, the teaching staffs in our schools have increasing value. We have to recognise this by providing the necessary support and training programmes. To identify whether your school is moving in the right direction check your accreditation with Investors In People (IIP). If the school is already an approved Investor, check your staff training programmes. If it is not, register with the scheme and begin the preparation needed to become accredited. Although involving paperwork, the scheme is designed to show that your organisation recognises the value of all staff and is actively seeking to provide the necessary training and support to meet the demands of individuals and the school.

TASK 41

Professional development

Find out from your local IIP representative, probably based at either the Education Business Partnership or at the local Learning and Skills Centre, for the names of two organisations that have achieved outstanding reports when they were accredited or re-accredited. Then arrange to visit them and speak to the staff training manager about their staff support and training programmes. Take the best ideas and implement them in your school.

Introducing a modular culture

The process required to achieve a modular culture has been described in detail in Chapters 4 and 6 from the perspective of the student. However, staff, especially teachers, have to live the culture too. This means changing teacher attitudes. It seems trite to say that teachers are increasingly becoming facilitators but this is the process that is happening. In a modular culture teachers have to hand over a significant amount of authority that has traditionally been in their hands. How does this come about?

To invite students to discuss how they, the students, will learn is often totally alien to a traditional classroom teacher. It can also be difficult for them to discuss how the work will be assessed. Most difficult of all can be the negotiation of grades, as many teachers do not readily invite a challenge to their professional judgement by their students. However, the learning that the student gains is his or hers, not the teacher's. In an age of individualism when everyone is in control of their own destiny, it seems out of place for schools not to move with the rest of society and educate young people to be able to make their own decisions about their learning. For too long we have assumed that just because of the attitude 'I've been through all my notes so the students must know the whole syllabus', then they really must know it. What is more, we then expect them to understand and apply the knowledge without much extra help. Some of people have always been able to do this, but now that we need 80 per cent at least of each generation to be able to do this, we have to provide a more relevant support structure for all. Staff need training and support to get used to a learning cycle of six weeks with discussion at the beginning and review and reflection at the end.

Difficulties arise when the teacher's dignity is built around their authority or charisma. In other words, if the teacher has been in control of his or her classroom and gained the respect of students simply by being authoritarian or charismatic, rather than having a depth of knowledge or being a good teacher, they will have their foundations as a 'teacher' undermined.

Recognising such individuals is not always easy and supporting and retraining them can prove extremely difficult. The following is a suggested list of characteristics:

■ strong disciplinarian

■ charismatic classroom performer

■ held in high regard by many students

■ intransigent with more senior staff

■ if charismatic, often attracts the more rebellious students

■ poor examination results (when using value added data).

Providing the last characteristic is missing and so long as the intransigence is not too subversive, then such characters can be a positive benefit to a staff. However, they will always need very careful managing. As soon as one or both of the aforementioned traits becomes prevalent, then action will be needed. The difficulty arises when these teachers are not prepared to make any attempt to change the way they work.

Professional development

Schools have always been knowledge organisations and now they have to step up a level in terms of the knowledge they provide. No longer is it acceptable for teachers just to teach students within the age range of the school. As a good employer the school needs to offer staff other opportunities. Examples of these would be as follows:

■ Provide support to staff starting higher degrees, such as Masters programmes or doctorates; it may be possible for university staff to come to the school to teach or for the local university to validate your training courses as credits towards higher degrees.

■ Provide adult education programmes to which your staff are encouraged to contribute. Potential developments would be that some staff would work part-time at school and part-time with adults.

■ Become part of a school-based initial teacher training (SCITT) consortium so that your staff can act as tutors and mentors to student teachers.

■ ICT training funded by NOF should be in operation. If it has finished, further training in ICT should be built into the school's staff training programme. Remember: to get the best out of the IT equipment purchased, the same amount of money should be spent on training.

The leading and managing of staff has thus far been supportive, but whilst these programmes are being established it is necessary to look at basic professional standards and ensure that these are known and followed by all the staff. It is quite remarkable at times to observe the standards that some junior colleagues consider acceptable.

TASK 42

Characteristics of good teachers

Refer to the characteristics of good classroom teachers as identified by Hay Mcber and listed at the end of Chapter 6, then write down the key points that all teachers should follow in their day-to-day interaction with young people. Then ask your senior staff to do this exercise. Draw up an agreed list and make sure it goes in the new staff induction handbook.

Performance management

With the advent of the Green Paper on teaching reforms and now with the introduction of Threshold Assessment and Performance Management, the need for rigorous and fair appraisal of the work of our staffs has become paramount. Up until now a great deal of the assessment of teachers had been nepotistic, hierarchical or even random. The only formal recognition of staff was when the Head promoted someone internally and frequently the criteria were not clear. The advent of the new process, even if it takes time to introduce, should make the recognition of good performance of staff a structured and fairer process. It will hold middle and senior management to account much more and we will have to make sure that we can meet the demands which the scheme will bring.

The process is now well underway for the first and second phases with all Heads having the opportunity to be trained to introduce the scheme. Despite the speed of change the underlying principles seem to make a lot of sense. In summary they could be stated as follows.

There is to be a formal process that seeks to find evidence to show that the professional teacher is carrying out all of his or her duties after working for some years and then to pay them more for doing so. Subsequently there will be further opportunities for the teacher to show that he or she is carrying out the duties to a higher standard and for this there will be greater financial reward.

Discipline issues

Despite your best efforts there will be times when a quiet word here and the odd reprimand there are not sufficient. Some staff insist on ploughing their own furrow rather than becoming part of the team. Others get drawn into actions that can only be described as misconduct. Others again, despite all the support that is provided, show that there are significant doubts about their competence. Finally there are those who commit acts that can only be described as gross misconduct.

Dealing with the last is usually the most straightforward. When the evidence is clear, action can be taken straight away, but always check your discipline and grievance procedures before starting formal disciplinary action and always check with the LEA or personnel support company. It is also likely that your insurance company will ask you to check with their legal helpline before taking action. The insurance company will want to be sure that your proposed action has the support of the legal profession, otherwise you may find that your insurance won't cover the action and the process could be very expensive.

For less serious offences it is important to follow procedures to be sure that all parties affected have a fair chance to put their case.

The guidelines to follow when managing a disciplinary situation should include the following:

- check with the LEA or personnel support, or your own professional association
- contact the insurance company
- contact the legal helpline
- keep a written record of everything
- circulate notes of meetings to all attendees
- make sure that there is sufficient clear-cut evidence and not hearsay
- ensure that the member of staff is properly represented
- consider all the options before taking action
- consider all the costs and disruption before taking action
- offer support to the member of staff at each point in the process
- arrange a 'without prejudice' meeting with the member of staff and his or her (union) representative before a formal meeting

- if the incident is serious, suspension of the member of staff is likely to be appropriate

- in a very difficult situation consider a 'compromise agreement' as a way forward

- don't rush into action. Never has the proverb 'Act in haste and repent at leisure' been more fitting than when dealing with staff disciplinary issues.

Being proactive

Much of the Head's time is spent in dealing with staff, so it pays to give due care and attention to them. Other tasks that should be done include:

- observing lessons regularly, particularly if you have chosen not to teach

- reading up on employment law and the Children's Act (1995)

- reading the staff files to find out about the background of the staff you inherit

- meeting regularly with staff representatives

- finding three staff each day to praise because of the high quality of their work or because of their dedication and commitment or because of the quality of the students' work that they are responsible for.

Summary

Our intention is that, at the end of this chapter, you will have:

- identified the competencies of your staff at an early stage of headship

- completed a skills audit of all staff to identify training needs

- devised a scheme to make performance management work positively for your school

- set the boundaries unambiguously and publicised them widely to all staff

- recognised that discipline issues will arise that require careful action and wide consultation and that fair handling of discipline issues requires consistency in all actions and the meticulous recording of events and comments

- learnt to apply the mantra 'public praise, private reprimand' and realise that everyone deserves their dignity.

chapter twelve

Financial management

Introduction

The aim of this chapter is to show how to use the finances to maximise the educational benefit to students' learning.

This chapter emphasises and attempts to develop some of the concepts in Brian Knight's outstanding work on this subject: *Financial Management for Schools*. This text is very readable and extremely sound and it would make no sense to repeat large sections of it here.

TASK 43

Financial management

Read *Financial Management for Schools* by Brian Knight and keep it readily available during your tenure as Head.

It may be very obvious, but without sound financial management you will be able to achieve nothing of lasting value and will soon be looking for another job. Without sufficient funds you cannot pay the wages or the bills and certainly you cannot make any significant changes to the structure of the school you inherit. This is the chapter where the Head changes into the chief executive. Brian Knight suggests that there is a range of roles that can be taken by the school leader, which are the same as described earlier in this book, with such titles as headteacher, principal or chief executive. It is our contention that in the successful school of tomorrow, the only way to tackle financial management is for the Head to be the chief executive.

What does this mean? It means understanding how the leader of a private company with a similar number of employees as your school has staff, carries out the financial management function successfully.

The school as a business

All businesses, and as we have said already, education is a business today, have to at least balance the books and it helps to make some profit. Schools have always taken the rather altruistic and blinkered view that somehow they were not businesses. It has generally been true that schools have not been in the business of making money profits for shareholders or executives, but they are in the business of making money for better educational facilities and they are in the business of making educational profits for their students. It would seem that we will be moving into an era when making financial profits out of the educational business is acceptable. It does sound increasingly naïve to think that it was quite acceptable for computer companies, publishers and printers, amongst others, to be able to make money out of schools, but not for the school itself to engage in anything so sordid as trade.

If we wish to maximise the educational opportunities for our young people then what is wrong with a school having part of its educational business as a money-making operation? We suggest nothing, provided the profits are used to enhance educational provision for the community.

Financial principles

The financial principles of any business are simple:

- there is an income line and an expenditure line
- as long as expenditure is less than income then the organisation can survive or flourish
- the income line has to be maximised
- the expenditure line has to be minimised
- this produces the maximum 'profit' that can be used for all the exciting projects that you want to implement.

The actual reality is obviously much more complex. If, however, these fundamental principles are known and understood, you have a chance of being able to stay in control of the school.

The key to success lies in maximising income and minimising unnecessary overheads. Again, there are no magic formulae, but following basic principles helps.

TABLE 12.1 Financial management – principles

- The need to have a clear vision based on philosophy and principles.

- A sound business plan should be in place.

- Access to regular financial expertise should be available.

- There should be sound financial practices followed within the organisation.

- There needs to be a focus on efficiency and effectiveness.

- The development plan should be linked to budgets.

- There should be a sharp focus on outcomes linked to input and process.

- There should be a capacity for lateral thinking.

Developing a business plan

Apart from considering the school development plan it is good practice also to write a business plan for the school.

There are many ways of finding out about business management. A visit to speak to your local small business adviser at one of the banks or the local Chamber of Commerce, or a study of the Young Enterprise company programme, which may well already be operating in the school, are sound starting points. (The YE website address is: young-enterprise.org.uk/.) You may also wish to speak to the business studies department of your school or to one of your governors, particularly if any have been successful in business.

TASK 44

Writing a business plan

Write a business plan for your school.

- Talk to your bursar/finance officer, Business Studies department, business governors, Chamber of Commerce, small business section of one of the local banks or your Young Enterprise connection.

- Carry out a SWOT analysis with the senior staff and governors of the financial issues relating to the school. SWOT stands for Strengths, Weaknesses, Opportunities and Threats. The process is well described in Brian Knight's book and many others on school planning. This will create the outline of the plan. It will take some months to fill in all the details and refine it so that it becomes a strategic and action plan for the business part of the school. Like other plans it will need auditing, reviewing and rewriting on a suitable cycle.

Now let us return to the fundamental principles. Consider all the outgoings and find ways of reducing them. One strategy that forces you both to realise what the essentials are and to prioritise them, is to consider what you would retain in your school if you only had half the income you now receive. You still have to deliver the best possible education to the same number of students and saying 'it can't be done' is not an option. The process enables you to identify and list in order a set of clear priorities. It is worth retaining this list and when financial times get tough bring this list out to guide the budget-cutting process.

When this is complete you have identified your core business and the essential costs to maintain a viable education programme.

———— Reducing overheads ————

To find ways of reducing costs requires considerable imagination and energy but it is quite remarkable what can be achieved. Obtain as detailed a breakdown of expenditure as possible and use this as the basis from which to work. Table 12.1 lists some common cost areas where controls are not always as rigorous as they perhaps should be and which could benefit from inspection and more rigorous monitoring. Staff costs have been left out of the list as they are treated separately later.

TABLE 12.2 Areas of expenditure which may be reducible

- photocopying
- waste paper at printers
- lighting and heating controls
- ventilation controls
- technology costs
- supply teacher costs
- telephone costs
- electricity, gas and oil costs
- cleaning charges
- school meals service
- school minibus

- text book collection
- loss of library books
- insurance costs

Staff costs

Since, on average, staff costs make up something over 75% of the budget, and in some schools significantly over 80%, this is the area to concentrate your attention on when considering expenditure.

Is it possible to reduce these costs and still retain a low pupil/teacher ratio? In posing such a question we have already made assumptions based on existing values. The paradigm within which we currently work in schools is creaking at the edges. The shift that is likely to come soon will almost certainly make such statements irrelevant. So there are two questions to answer, what do we do *now* and what will the new paradigm be?

The answer to the first is to consider what really matters to your school. If pupil/teacher ratios really matter, then use this as a basis for the next set of decisions. If, however, there are other ways that students are organised involving technicians and classroom assistants, then perhaps the question is already meaningless. In this situation a better question might be: 'How do we maximise the time that each student has with a teacher and other adults each week for minimum financial cost?' The answer to this is in someone's crystal ball. The hints at what it might be are bound up with many factors that include:

- use of other staff – teachers and classroom assistants – in schools
- links to other adults via distance learning
- cost of the new technology
- income available from government
- structure of education in the future.

Accounting for expenditure

Whilst expenditure is being kept under control it will also pay to consider how to account for expenditure. Costs fall into two categories: revenue and capital. Choosing which category to place a purchase such as computers in can be quite instructive. It has been customary in education to account for equipment purchases as revenue, taking no account of lifespan. But computers have a life of at least three years, possibly five and some last longer than that but they have little value then. If we capitalise the cost of the equipment we can then take due account of depreciation and build the cost into future budgets so that we can replace items at the appropriate time without having to scramble around for money.

For example, if a computer system costs £900 per unit and will have a useful life of three years we need to 'put aside' £300 pounds a year to cover the cost of replacement in three years' time. Schools have been reluctant to do this. Whilst the Funding Agency for Schools started the process of asset accounting, as it is called, in the two years before its demise, the practice has not yet become widespread. The practice has been started by the Department for Education and Employment in respect of City Technology Colleges and it requires that all assets – land and buildings as well – are properly accounted for in the balance sheet. This gives rise to some frightening statements of accounts if you are not used to this method of accounting – they show some large negative numbers. But it has the effect of making sure that the Head and governors are fully aware of the assets they control and the costs of maintaining them in relation to the revenue budgets they manage. Thus we need to ensure that all budget holders pay due regard to replacement costs and that they account for them in their spending plans. It should then be possible to build up sufficient reserves over a period of time to meet the cost of capital equipment items from revenue so that the school does not have to go cap in hand to the LEA, government, school board every time it needs to replace its computers, milling machines or minibuses. It will take some years to achieve but we suggest that it would be a good target to aim for in the school's long-term planning.

Government is not going to continue to hand out largesse forever and as we have seen in recent years schools increasingly have to find financial resources for themselves. This then leads into the second major part of financial management that has to be considered – increasing the income. It is only by raising extra income that it will be possible to balance the books as we move to asset accounting in schools.

_____ Maximising income _____

There are no secrets here. There are currently five sources of income for a school which have to be maximised and each school has to decide how it will tackle the issues it faces.

1 Revenue grant from government/LEA.

2 Capital funds from bids to LEA or central government or even PFI (private finance initiative) sources.

3 Bids to various government funding bodies and to European funds.

4 Sponsorship from private companies.

5 Make your own money!

To begin the process tackle the following task.

TASK 45

Increasing revenue

- With the senior staff and governors, brainstorm possible ways of increasing your revenue stream.

- Group the ideas together and pursue any that might be promising. Remember the core business is education and training. Take note of the expertise that can be called on from governors and that might reside within the skills of existing staff. What are the local business needs? Continue to ask the questions and probe for answers.

We think you might wish to consider the following:

- increasing student numbers, but remember that this is not always beneficial financially (see Knight, p.113)

- applying for specialist school status

- setting up a trading company to sell ICT, training or other services to the community and business

- bidding to become part of a European project

- considering joining with a group of schools to bid for PFI funding to rebuild all the schools because either they cost too much to maintain or because the way you wish to use teaching and learning spaces has changed so radically that you need to completely rebuild your school

- develop such an exciting vision of the school that your local philanthropists wish to sponsor the school to help you achieve it.

When you have found a range of ideas you will need to link them to the business plan. This should help to prioritise them. As many as can be afforded, in both financial and human terms, should be started. This is the point at which the judgement of the chief executive is crucial, as you have the clearest vision of what the organisation can manage at any one time. It is unlikely that ten new activities will start up at once but the statistics on the development of new ideas suggest that six out of ten new ideas/projects fail, three will succeed partially and no more than one will succeed. This area seems to be one where it is not possible to teach the right way, it is only possible to learn by experience. This means that there will be some failures and moreover it seems that it is essential that there are some for learning to occur.

When that good idea begins to take effect it is quite likely that it will come from an unexpected source, unless you can afford large sums to pay for marketing experts to identify needs. But even they are rarely able to spot that elusive 'gap in the market'.

CASE STUDY

Three years ago a school had deficit on its profit and loss account of over £100,000. It has now an expected surplus of over £30,000 in the current year with no debts, no staff have been made redundant and there is the prospect of greater surpluses in future years. The actions taken to achieve this have included:

- increasing student numbers both pre-16 and post 16
- reviewing contracts for gas, oil, electricity, cleaning and catering
- redefining insurance
- increasing trading activities in lettings of rooms, sports facilities, etc.
- increasing trading activities in printing and DTP
- starting an IT support business for local schools
- beginning training courses for adults and small and medium enterprises (SMEs).

At least three ideas have failed and no activity is yet making large amounts of money.

Other factors which have undoubtedly helped are:

- redefinition of the mission and aims of the school
- writing a ten-year development plan
- being amongst the 100 most improved schools in England in terms of examination success at 16
- having a regular positive profile in the local media – success always breeds success
- being significantly oversubscribed for applications into the school.

———— Summary ————

Our intention is that, at the end of this chapter, you will have:

- understood that education is and always has been a business
- learnt that schools should have a business plan as well as a development plan
- analysed ways of maximising your income by looking at all opportunities which include: lettings, training, selling expertise, grant applications, bidding
- devised ways of minimising overheads by cutting out wastage wherever possible
- scrutinised staff deployment as staff are the most expensive resource and have to be utilised wisely and to maximum educational benefit.

chapter thirteen

Value added education

Introduction

The purpose of this chapter is to show the power of facts and figures to help raise achievement in a school and to raise the expectations of both staff and students. The raising of expectations is one of the most important aspects of the job of the school leader because we have found that it is one of the most critical of all factors in school improvement. There are so many Jeremiahs out there that evidence is needed to counter them.

If you collect all the numerical data on your school that you can and then compare it with

- the data on other similar schools,
- the data on other schools that you are seeking to emulate,

it can be a very powerful lever in raising educational achievement when used in the right way. What this chapter does not do is explain in detail how to carry out the statistical work on the data (there are plenty of texts out there already, e.g. *Measuring Education: Quality, Indicators and Effectiveness* by Carol Fitz-Gibbon), but it does suggest ways of interpreting the results and how to use this with staff and students.

The ways suggested here are some of the ways that have been found to work. They have been found to be effective in a variety of educational settings in different countries. The technique, which is also called benchmarking, comes from industrial practice and one of its great strengths is its capacity to take personalities out of failure. It can achieve this because the focus is on collecting data and not on subjective judgements or anecdotal evidence. Even though this may point at an individual the data seems to encourage the user to support the individual and to seek out more fundamental causes.

What data should be collected?

There are two types of data on your school:

- educational achievement data
- institutional data.

Then there is the data that you collect for comparators through standardised tests and from published sources that aggregate individual data and carry out analysis on it. Data available here comes from many sources:

- DfEE examination performance tables
- Key Stage 1, 2 and 3 data
- PICSI and PandA data from Ofsted
- Ofsted reports
- standardised tests such as Nelson Cognitive Abilities Tests – CATs on verbal and non-verbal reasoning skills
- ALIS, YELLIS and MIDYIS from the CEM centre at Durham University run by Carol Fitz-Gibbon
- *Adding up the Sums* from the National Audit Office which compares school spending across the country.

There will be many other sources that relate to specific aspects of the organisation, but trying to use too much data can be as ineffective as using too little. This is an important point. Before swamping your staff and students with data, check how much data are used at present and in what ways before introducing any more. If there is very little used at present only introduce the data in small amounts as there is a cultural change of attitude required within the organisation.

Educational achievement data

The data that you have comes from various sources some of which are internal and some external and which can also be classified as 'hard' and 'soft'. Hard data are actual results and known facts, such as census data. Soft data – internal data – include teacher assessments and estimations, marks and grades from internal examinations. Some of the external data are soft data too: the information from ALIS and YELLIS, and CAT scores that allows predictions to be made. Other external data are hard, such as results from public examinations from Key Stage 1 to A-level. So too is the PICSI information and much of the PandA data (but not that based on free school meals!). The analysis of the school's results against the prediction data from YELLIS and ALIS is also hard since it gives firm indications of how students in your school have performed against national expectations. The hard data are the measure of outcomes and the soft data help prediction and expectation.

In August and September schools use the hard data to analyse actual results. Each individual teacher's performance is then looked at against the overall school results and subject leaders and senior staff will discuss the outcomes individually.

The next task is to look at the predictions for the coming academic year and revise the estimates of performance if any significant factors emerge from the analysis. It is crucial to identify positive signs and highlight them; it is also crucial to find negative sign and to identify ways of minimising or eliminating their impact. General statements, such as 'this is a terrible year group coming through, they have always been trouble, we are bound to have a dip in performance next year' must not be allowed to take hold. The year group may well have a number of difficult students in it but unless that attitude is stopped in its tracks, then a downward spiral will commence from which it will be increasingly difficult to climb out. Find the good signs, there will be plenty of them, decide on some strategies that will help and identify the key students to turn. By that we mean that in every group of students there are natural leaders and influential individuals. Identify these, they usually stand out, and work on them. Use senior staff and parents to support. Use any mentoring system that the school has, bring in successful local business people to act as mentors to help change:

- self image
- self esteem
- self respect which in turn will change:
  - attitude to learning and life
  - motivation to learn.

Students have to learn that they can take control of their lives and that they can influence what happens to them. Having the opportunity to meet and talk to senior staff and significant local people raises their self esteem and can help to break the cycle of rejection that many teenagers fall into in adolescence.

Using value added data in mentoring

One of the greatest motivating factors that we have come across here is the use of the value added data in mentoring discussions, which can be with the form tutor or a senior member of staff or another adult. *The data needs to be made available to students as fully as possible and as soon as possible.* Young people are extremely astute and they know when they are being hoodwinked and patronised. They like to know how well they are really doing and what they have to do to get better. Pretending otherwise quickly leads to rejection and disparagement of the 'system'.

Data required

- Last year's final examination results
- analysis of previous years' results
- previous performance by individual students during their time at school
- current performance data by the student being mentored
- predictions by staff of likely examination performance
- predictions by student of likely examination performance.

Leading the session

Questions and statements to be used to lead the mentoring session are suggested below.

- Consider current performance, ask the student if he or she is satisfied with it.
- Is this performance good enough?
- Can it get better?
- How well do you think you can do in you in the examinations? Refer to student's predictions.
- Is this good enough?
- Are you aware that your teachers think that you can achieve ...? Refer to teacher predictions.
- Previously there have been students with the same sort of performance as you. On average they have achieved 'x'. The best students have gone on to achieve 'y' and the poorest performance has been 'z'. (Use the school data that will have been analysed similarly to that in Table 13.1.)
- Now, how well do you really think you can do?

The discussion then moves on to learning strategies to achieve these goals.

Session outcome

When the mentoring discussions have finished students should know their key targets and learning strategies to achieve their own predicted results, modified or raised as the case may be. Their teachers should know what the students' predictions are and which subjects they need to make a special effort in.

Some of the school data that are of most value when used with students are shown in Tables 13.1 and 13.2.

TABLE 13.1 Data for use with GCSE students in Years 10 and 11

Key Stage 3 scores (sum of E, M, Sc. levels)	Average GCSE point score	Best results	Worst results
Students with 21+ achieved	66	96	58
18–20	60	80	40
15–17	55	65	36
12–14	42	53	29
9–11	35	40	18
<9	27	38	8

TABLE 13.2 Examination performance over time – value added links

Measure	Value in 2000	Value in 1999	Value in 1998	Value in 1997
Average stanine score in Y7 (3 added together)	16	15	14	13
Average stanine score in Y9	17	16	15	14
KS3 average score in E, M, Sc added together	18	17	16	15
Average GCSE point score	45	44	43	42
Staff prediction of point score	43	44	42	40
Student prediction of point score	48	48	46	44
% students with 5 A*-C	66	63	56	54
Predicted % for 5 A*-C	60	58	56	54

From Table 13.2 we can immediately see that students achieved higher results than expected in 1999 and rather worse than expected in 1998, according to earlier data. The crucial points to take from this data are:

- analyse the results to find the reasons for differences from expectations both above and below
- use the better than expected results to raise expectations further for the next year.

There are few students who can resist the challenge to outsmart their predecessors. They will engage in the discussion and will not want to be a statistic next year that shows that they have set a new all time low performance. Increasingly they will also expect to achieve the average performance and the good students will seek to beat the best from previous years. The process creates a positive cycle to learning and can lead to year on year improvement, since most students in each cohort expect to achieve the average and many strive to do better. Consequently the average performance goes up each year. Greenhead Sixth Form College in Huddersfield has been using a system similar to this with post 16 students for many years and its examination results are among the very best of all 16–18 colleges in the country, far in excess of what might be expected from its intake.

When the data are available for the current year the analysis can be further refined. The breakdown and analysis that is available from the CEM centre in Durham on ALIS and YELLIS data arrives during the year and provides a second chance to review performance targets and refine the school's thinking on how to enable each student to achieve her or his very best in the next year. Additional mentoring sessions can then be held, with a final session after the mock examinations.

TASK 46

Value added data analysis

1 Review the value added data that is collected in your school or decide what value added data to collect.

2 Review the mentoring system that is in place in your school, if it exists.

3 Create a new mentoring process that integrates mentoring and value added data.

4 Prepare and train staff to make full use of the new system, then implement it.

When combined with the modular learning culture described earlier, the majority of students gain the habit of regularly reviewing their performance and actively seeking ways to get better.

Institutional data

Institutional data are data on your organisation that have a bearing on value added education, but are focused on general attitudes to school and life. The data are gained from the key performance indicators that the school has identified. These were discussed in Chapter 8. Obviously attendance rates have an impact on educational outcomes, especially for students from disadvantaged backgrounds. It is also straightforward to say that reducing vandalism will have a positive impact on learning since less money spent on repairs means more money available for resources.

We would also contend that there are crucial factors that affect examination standards such as the amount of litter and chewing gum in an environment. It should be a constant target for reduction and elimination. The quality of the environment is critical to the sense of well being and value that students have and place in their school. Their sense of ownership rises and hence their motivation. The way students speak to each other as well as the way they speak to teachers is critical, because it shows how much respect each person shows to others. This can be measured by the number of violent incidents and bullying incidents as well as the number of times teachers report abuse towards themselves.

Although only a short note at the end of this section, we cannot stress how important it is to pay due regard to the small details of school life and to measure them in your basket of performance indicators with the intention of reducing the negative ones to a minimum.

Summary

Our intention is that, at the end of this chapter, you will have:

- realised that numerical data hold the key to raising performance and that it is essential to gather as much as you can and analyse it carefully
- learnt that numerical data can take the personalities out of failure
- understood that it is important to integrate the data analysis with mentoring of students in raising student and staff expectations
- recognised that institutional data are an important indicator of the health of your learning environment.

chapter fourteen

Updating comprehensive schools

Specialist schools

The specialist schools concept came to life in 1987 with the establishment of the first City Technology Colleges (CTCs). Since the original 15 were established the concept has been widened to the specialist schools programme which now encompasses around 500 schools. There are a further 400 schools affiliated to the Technology Colleges Trust which has the duty of managing the programme. In the first instance the project was about trying out new ways of delivering education in difficult areas where current methods had failed. All the CTCs have now shown success in transforming education in their areas; some have done so quite spectacularly. There are now Language, Arts and Sports Colleges as well as Technology Colleges. The concept is successfully transforming levels of achievement. The work of David Jesson, *Value-added in Specialist Schools*, shows statistically reliable evidence for the significant extra improvement that has taken place during the past five years in specialist schools. Jesson appears to show that the improvement goes beyond the extra resources and he identifies seven factors, many of which we have already raised in other parts of the book:

- the bidding process sharpens the school's understanding of the improvement process

- focus on achievement – schools use imaginative techniques to get students to 'focus on their own achievement'

- target setting – as a result of building a culture of target setting, schools develop an ethos of high expectations and valuing high achievement

- sponsor governors – there is an increase in the external focus of the school provided by sponsor governors

- enhanced provision and facilities – the extra resources can create a 'buzz' and be a stimulus to changes of attitudes to learning. All subjects benefit from this, not just those of the specialism.

- reorganising the school day and year – specialist schools have taken the lead in breaking the mould of accepted patterns of schooling. The five term year, the fixed year and breakfast clubs are among the initiatives that started in specialist schools

- vision and leadership – it is the use to which extra funds are put that counts and it is the quality of the vision and leadership that allows this.

We strongly advise any new Head to seek affiliation to the Technology Colleges Trust, even if there is no intention to become a specialist school. The network of Heads in these schools is very strong and very supportive. It is also collaborative and positive in outlook.

Increasingly now, those schools that have had specialist status for more than three years are seeking ways to challenge existing norms. It is this support in developing your personal boldness that helps to drive forward change in your own organisation. Even if no one has yet tried your latest idea, you can be almost certain that there will be others who have thought about it too. If you discuss the changes with them you may find that there will be two or three schools planning and implementing the change together. Staffs from the different schools start to make networks and soon the momentum is unstoppable. You have now taken much of the risk out of the bold action you were planning.

The other function that specialist schools have had to take on as part of their status is that they have to support other schools within their local community and spread their expertise around. The expertise is now starting to cross boundaries other than those between schools. Health and social services providers and libraries are forging ever closer links with schools and in some cases have completely amalgamated their functions to, what appears to be, the benefit of their communities. Consequently the government target of 25% of all secondary schools having specialist status is to be applauded.

Education Action Zones and Excellence in Cities

It is still too early to report on success in these initiatives, but as a Head it is valuable for you to follow their development and find out the new ideas that are being trialled here. The programmes have taken the best of the specialist schools scheme and added a number of extras.

The DfEE guidelines on best practice taken from their website suggest that they are looking for:

'Local partnerships to put forward their own radical and imaginative proposals to raise standards. The best initiatives will probably share a number of broad characteristics:

■ strong leadership from the head and senior staff, pursuing rigorous and determined programmes of school improvement;

■ shared responsibility for the pupil's learning by their families and by the pupils themselves, with participation in school life and support for its aims;

■ partnership with a range of wider support agencies. The voluntary, community and business sectors have a long history of enhancing education in their neighbourhoods;

■ a sharp focus on teaching and learning, with extra-curricular activities to broaden the educational experience;

■ innovation and flexibility in curriculum organisation and delivery, and in staffing;

■ high and consistent expectations of pupils, reflected by challenging and achievable targets and action plans, with opportunities for early, measurable success;

■ monitoring of pupil progress;

■ a good atmosphere or spirit including rewards and incentives for pupils to succeed;

■ educational and other measures to address low attendance and high pupil mobility.'

Again the same kind of targets and processes that all schools are seeking to achieve are here. We should not expect spectacular success overnight as it takes time to change culture and embed an ethos of achievement. It will take about five years for significant change to be noticed and secure. It took the CTCs at least that long to achieve significant success. Nonetheless, the agenda on raising standards has never had such political momentum behind it and Michael Barber, in a recent speech in Washington D.C., said in answer to a question about how he saw the learning environment in 2005:

'I would sum it up as a learning environment in which:

■ the school system and all who work in it are committed to high expectations for every pupil;

■ *this commitment is pursued through a focus on the needs and aspirations of pupils, instead of a presumption that pupils have to fit into the system;*

■ *teachers have this commitment at the heart of their professional ethos;*

■ *teachers use a range of ways to focus on pupils' needs, including radically new approaches to pedagogy based on new technology and on collaboration with skilled education paraprofessionals;*

■ *while schools will remain crucial and provide the foundation of learning, they will also seek learning opportunities outside, and take on the roles of advocates for pupils and guarantors of quality, instead of sole providers of education.'*

So the Excellence in Cities programme and the Beacon Schools programme are all designed to focus on raising achievement, especially in deprived areas. So wherever you are a Head or wherever you wish to become one, there are very strong supportive structures to which you can align your school to maximise the impact that your tenure will bring.

The latest announcement of the City Academies programme is yet another initiative designed to speed the access of our most deprived young people to a positive learning culture and an ethos of high expectation.

———— Summary ————

Our intention is that, at the end of this chapter, you will have:

■ become aware that the specialist schools programme is making a significant difference to the lives of thousands of our citizens

■ learnt that specialist schools now spread their expertise into their communities

■ realised that the new programmes of Action Zones, Excellence in Cities, Beacon Schools and City Academies are all designed to be inclusive and to allow as many of our young people to benefit from the success of earlier programmes as possible

■ seen that the new schemes are also expected to maximise the use of new technology in their learning programmes

■ decided that your school should seek to emulate or join one of the programmes.

chapter fifteen

Working with governors

Introduction

One of the areas for which you will have had least preparation when you become Head is working with governors. This chapter focuses on learning how to manage your relationship with the governing body.

The relationship between the Head and governors

In talking to colleagues it is obvious that getting this relationship right and maintaining it is often one of the most difficult parts of being a Head. However good the governing body is, there are two aspects that need constant revisiting to maintain a good relationship. As ever, they are communication and understanding. Each governor has an agenda beyond the relationship to the school and you cannot actually direct governors nor, in many aspects of your daily life, can they tell you what to do. You can only advise them and much of the time they only want to advise you. You can easily appreciate that it would be impossible to retain your job if the governing body were having to direct you to take action!

Almost all Heads speak highly of their governing bodies and warmly praise their work. All Heads also comment on the difficulties that they have incurred with one or more governors at different times. Mostly they are well intentioned but sometimes, sadly, they are not. This part of the job has been likened to trying to 'herd cats'.

The dilemma and the difficulties arise from the tension that exists between the two roles. Conflict occurs when someone oversteps his or her role in the eyes of the other. Many governors see their role as being powerful, which it usually isn't. Perhaps the chairman has power, but certainly the other governors on their own, do not. However, governors do have responsibility for the proper management of the school and they do have responsibility for ensuring that educational policies and practice are within the law. They have to monitor the practices of the Head and the leadership team to ensure that they are acting reasonably. The liability is mostly invested in the Head unless the governors are the employer. So the power and authority that governors have enables them to hold the Head to account, but not to enable them to take executive action. If the Head cannot convince the governors of the need for a change of policy, he or she will get frustrated and then disillusioned. The relationship thus needs constant work and we cannot stress too highly how important this task is.

The most frequent description of the relationship found in the literature is that the governor – and especially the chairman – is the 'critical friend' of the Head. The Head by definition is the 'Chief Executive Officer' of the Board of Governors. The area of dispute arises because so few of the 'Board' have detailed expertise of schools and too few have any experience of being on the board of a company. Most adults take the view that because they went to school for ten years, they are an expert on how schools run. Most governors, who know nothing about schools, thus take such a view. Modern entrepreneurial business people know a great deal that can immediately be applied to schools and are often the best source of advice, support and 'critical friendliness'. It should be obvious why such individuals are so much support: it is because schools are, increasingly, a modern entrepreneurial business.

Defining the roles

What you need to do is define the roles that you expect of governors and the role you expect to take towards the governing body. This is defined in part by the vision you and the governors have for the school. The more 'school-like' the vision, the more tried and tested relationships will work, but your business governors will be frustrated. The more visionary and entrepreneurial your school, the better will be your relationship with the business governors, but the LEA and community governors will feel increasingly isolated and frustrated.

Much of what follows has been taken from a paper prepared by the Audit Commission and Ofsted to assist governors called: 'Lessons in Teamwork'. We have added to it and sometimes summarised it here.

The most effective governing bodies are those which:

- *agree the distinctive roles of the governing body and the headteacher*
- *Work together as a team, fostering a supportive, yet constructively critical, relationship with the Head*
- *improve their knowledge and experience through regular training*

- *develop their awareness of the community served by the school*
- *keep themselves informed about the standards of teaching and pupil achievement, using comparisons with other schools to put their own school's performance into context.*

The quality of leadership provided by the chair, the contribution of the Head and the administrative support provided by the clerk all help to determine whether the governing body makes an effective contribution to the life of the school. The work of the governing body will run smoothly if meetings are carefully planned with clear agendas that give appropriate priority to the most important issues. Matters that require more detailed consideration can be left to committee, which will be able to devote more time to them.

Becoming more effective

There are four issues to tackle to make your governing body and you as Head more effective:

- definition of the roles of governors, chair and Head and the boundaries between them
- working practices of the Head, chair, governors individually and the committees
- accountability
- influencing performance.

These need to be taken within the context of what type of organisation your school is becoming.

TASK 47

Governors' aims

Attempt to answer these three questions on your own. Next ask your chair of governors to answer them. Then discuss your responses with your chair of governors. Hopefully they won't be too different! This is best done as a light-hearted task when you are relaxing with your chair of governors at an easy moment.

1 What type of school is yours and what type of school are you becoming?

2 When did you and the governing body last consider your vision for the school?

3 Write down the two main aims of your governing body.

———— Defining the governing body's role ————

The main aim of the governing body is to maintain and improve the standard of education provided. It can be divided into five key areas.

1 *Steering:* agreeing the aims and values of the school; setting a policy on the curriculum, including any requirement for special education needs; setting budgets and approving school development plans; responding to official reports and, when necessary, publishing action plans in response.

2 *Monitoring:* making sure that the school adheres to its policies, budgets and plans; keeping informed about the quality and standards of education at the school, including pupil achievement.

3 *Executive:* taking direct responsibility for recruitment of senior staff and some disciplinary matters, while recognising the Head's responsibility for managing the school; contributing to the admissions policy and appeals system.

4 *Accountability:* making sure that parents are kept informed about what is happening in the school and that their views are taken into account.

5 *Support:* supporting and advising Heads by giving advice when necessary, usually this begins with financial advice; knowing when not to offer advice and when not to interfere.

FIG. 15.1 The differing roles of governing bodies

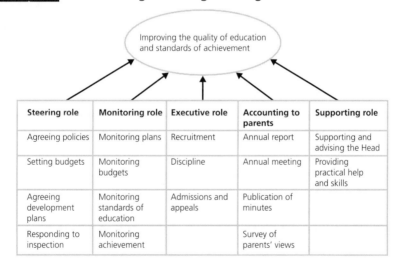

Steering role	Monitoring role	Executive role	Accounting to parents	Supporting role
Agreeing policies	Monitoring plans	Recruitment	Annual report	Supporting and advising the Head
Setting budgets	Monitoring budgets	Discipline	Annual meeting	Providing practical help and skills
Agreeing development plans	Monitoring standards of education	Admissions and appeals	Publication of minutes	
Responding to inspection	Monitoring achievement		Survey of parents' views	

One school's strategy for differentiating between the role of the Head and the role of the governors is shown in Table 15.1.

TABLE 15.1 Roles of governors and the Head

Area of responsibility	Governing body's role	Head's role
School aims and development plans	With the Head to: – agree aims and values of the school – approve and set priorities in the plan – monitor how the plan is implemented.	Preparing costed proposals for the development plan that are consistent with aims and priorities set by the governing body. Implementing the approved plan and reporting progress to the governing body.
Curriculum	Setting policy and ensuring that it reflects statutory requirements. Monitoring implementation of policy by the Head including at least annual consideration of the standards achieved by students	Determining and organising the detailed curriculum and assessment arrangements, including the use of resources, in line with the policy set by the governing body and by legislation. Monitoring the day-to-day delivery of the curriculum, including standards of teaching and learning.
Staffing	Deciding the staffing structure and numbers. Appointing the Head and deputies and agreeing how their work will be appraised. Making arrangements for a panel for disciplinary hearings and an appeals committee.	Taking delegated responsibility for all other appointments and promotions in line with the governing body's policies. Managing staff in accordance with the governing body policy including pay and conditions, staff appraisal, development and discipline.
Finance	Receiving, amending and approving the budget. Approving the annual accounts and setting limits on the use of surpluses (virement). Monitoring expenditure.	Managing the budget within guidelines set by the governing body. Ensuring financial procedures are correct and secure.
Charging	Setting policy.	Implementing policy.

TASK 48

Governing body responsibilities

1 Construct a matrix of roles and responsibilities for you and your governing body.

2 On a governors' training day, give your governing body the above matrix and ask them in pairs to construct one for the school, adding and subtracting duties as appropriate.

3 Compare the results and draw up an overarching list that will form the basis for the relationship between you and the governors for the next few years.

_____ Governors' training _____

TASK 49

Governors' training

Plan a series of training sessions with your governors during the first three years. Include time for:

- revisiting the vision
- roles of governors with respect to the difference between monitoring, review and inspection
- reviewing policies
- governor visits
- raising standards and the use of performance indicators and value added data.

Through a thorough programme of activities governors will rapidly increase their understanding of how the school operates and what precisely is the nature of the two roles. They will also gain confidence and trust in you. It makes the tough days that much easier to bear, knowing that you have the full support of your governing body.

Make available the following:

■ induction packs and courses for new governors

■ a visits programme to the school to see how it really works each day

- briefings and training courses
- information and professional advice services from outside agencies
- joint discussion forums with governors from other schools, possibly through the National Governors Association.

Information packs

TASK 50

Governor information packs

1 Draw up a list of items you would put in a governors' pack to be given to all new governors.

2 Check with your governors if the list is comprehensive enough or too comprehensive – too much paper is worse than too little! Modify as necessary and return to the contents of this file every few years.

3 Review your governors' pack every few years.

Your list of items may look a little different, but Table 15.2 below illustrates one way of formatting the table of contents.

TABLE 15.2 Example of contents of governors' information pack

Responsible committee	Document title	Date approved by resp. comm.	Date approved by full gov.	Next review date	Comments
FULL GOVERNORS	School mission	N/a	Feb. 2000	Feb. 2003	
FINANCE	Budget	Feb. 2000	Mar. 2000	Feb. 2001	
CURRICULUM	IT policy	Jun. 1999	Sept. 1999	Jun. 2001	
STAFF	Performance management	Jun. 2000	Sept. 2000	Jun. 2003	

Summary

Our intention is that, at the end of this chapter, you will have:

- learnt that it is easy to take governors for granted and that they need careful, regular nurturing
- realised that governors are your critical friends, not members of the executive
- seen that it is important that governors know and understand the mission of the school
- defined governor and Head responsibilities fully to leave minimum opportunity for dispute
- ensured that governors have sufficient training to carry out their duties
- developed an information file for governors.

chapter sixteen

Being the centre of the community

Introduction

Increasingly the school is being asked to be the focal point in the community or is becoming so by a process of osmosis. There are many reasons for this which are linked to the changes that are occurring in our society caused by globalisation and the social effects of technology. The school is the one place to which most local people still feel they have some allegiance as it is the one place in an area with which most local people tend to have a link, however far in the past it may have been. So rather than wait to have all the attention focused on the school, spend significant time finding out how it fits into the web of the local community. Try to understand how the national policy changes are likely to affect the relationship and then plan the role you think is appropriate for your school. When you have done this talk to all the relevant people. This is likely to include staff, governors, business organisations, local clubs, the health service and the library as well as any specialist groups that might be an integral part of your plans. These could be sports groups, arts groups, environmental groups or the local Chamber of Commerce.

Go out there into the community and offer your school's services to it. In this way you maintain control, are seen as a positive, active contributor and can manage events and circumstance rather than let things happen to you. This surely has to be the essential difference between the school of this century and the school of the last. We have to take an active leadership role rather than a passive one.

Working with your LEA

Establish the kind of relationship you want with the LEA officers. Many LEAs provide a very supportive structure for schools. However, in tomorrow's schools the emphasis is increasingly on the Head as independent leader, with the LEA as a support if needed and as a monitoring agent. For the present the LEA still controls the purse strings, but the perception is that local government is not the most effective way of transferring money to schools, nor do many of them appear to have the structure to respond fast enough in our ever more rapidly changing world. The direction in which financial and other controls are moving suggests that with more and more of the money going directly to schools they have the freedom to choose whether they wish to buy back services from the LEA or whether they prefer to buy them elsewhere. We have found among Heads an increasing intolerance of and frustration with their LEA in many areas, and the high profile inspections of authorities that have been giving damning reports has not helped their cause.

The paradigm shift that is yet to happen in local government will produce a different structure by which communities manage their affairs. It is as yet unclear what this will be, although the momentum at present suggests a very much reduced role for LEAs in school affairs. The Grant Maintained and City Technology Colleges experience has raised the legitimate question as to why the LEAs require between 20 per cent and 30 per cent of money for schools to deliver their part of the education service. These schools have managed to deliver a significantly improved education and better examination results compared with LEA schools when they had, or have in the case of CTCs, control of most or all of their budget.

If this is the direction then the Head has to take note of this trend and seek to maximise it to the advantage of the school. We suggest, therefore, that Heads should seek to find ways of reducing their dependence on their local authority and build partnerships within their immediate local community and amongst other colleagues.

The additional freedom and responsibility, as always, have to be balanced but the essence of the direction that education is taking is that more decisions can be taken locally and thus are based on providing the best possible educational service to your students in your environment. This gives you greater control of spending but it also makes you more responsible and more accountable – there are fewer opportunities to shift blame elsewhere.

Collaborative competition

One of the widely reported weaknesses or faults reported from the grant maintained era was the cut-throat competition that developed between schools, which led to a certain amount of distrust and, in some cases, isolation. This is not unusual in the development of a new market and when it reaches maturity this destructive competition will become collaborative competition. What does this mean and what does it look like?

As the schools market opens up and Heads and other staff become familiar with the operation, it becomes clear that cooperation in areas of common interest will benefit all the schools in an area. There will still be areas where they will compete but each will be able to be more successful if they cooperate in areas of common interest.

Examples of common interest are:

- joint sixth forms
- membership of the same School-based Initial Teacher Training scheme (SCITT)
- common admission arrangements at age five or 11
- shared staff development programmes
- shared peripatetic music staff
- joint arrangements for the transfer of difficult students between schools to prevent exclusion.

With a changing role for the LEA and greater independence it is possible to foresee groups of schools amalgamating, merging or even being taken over, which will create large or super schools such as already exist in Sweden. This would ensure that there could be different campuses with different specialisms, such as Arts, Languages and Technology at the secondary level, and there could be a group of primary campuses that would feed into them. This would create a set of school premises which had a similar culture and vision and similar standards, with one set of governors and which were directly responsible to the community. There would be a chief executive responsible overall and each site would have its own Head. The chief executive would be somewhere between a Head and County Education Officer from an educational perspective and would have similar responsibilities to the chief executive of a medium-sized enterprise financially, but be similar to a large enterprise in terms of employees.

Although this picture is speculative, pressure for fundamental change is building and the cries are being echoed around the developed world. As a Head it is important to be aware of the debate and to realise the impact it is having on the LEA officials with whom we have to work. Some develop a siege mentality and others roll up their sleeves and see the impending change as a chance to be in the vanguard of the remodelling of local government. It is important to know what kind of local authority you are working in and what type of approach officials and elected members take.

_____ Working with parents _____

Society has given greater choice to individuals over the past 20 years because technology has allowed it and driven the change. The advertisement that includes the phrase 'we are all bank managers now' touches a chord: we all have the capacity to be in charge of our own lives now in a way that was not possible before. In education it means that parents have choice, or at least can express a preference for the school of their choice, and with increasing curriculum content available through the media and the internet they have real choice about whether they send their children to school at all. As a Head therefore you have to take note and act accordingly.

Parents are made aware of what is happening in school in a number of ways and each way has to be used to get your message across and to listen to what parents are saying. Methods could include:

- individual letters home, both good and bad
- telephone
- children's tales
- parents' gossip
- e-mail
- Parent Teacher Association
- whole school letters and newsletters home
- media coverage: press, radio and television
- questionnaires
- web sites and e-mail.

The first five are individual communications and the last five are groups or whole school communications. The customer care programme that teachers and all other staff need to display today cannot be overestimated in its importance. The one-to-one interactions and follow up are the face of the school as the individual family and child know it. This image cannot be too distant from the public face of the school as portrayed by the wider communications. If it does become large, you as the Head have a credibility gap which damages your authority with one of your most important group of supporters.

Communicating with parents

1 Take each of the first five ways of communicating with parents and analyse each of them for your school. Look at style, content accuracy and follow up. If there is significant inconsistency, or the standards are much below what you consider to be acceptable, it may well pay to have part or all of a staff training day specifically devoted to customer care so that all staff realise the importance of communicating effectively with parents.

2 Take the five ways of communicating to whole groups and again analyse the content and the impact of the messages. Again look for inconsistencies and standards. Take action where necessary. Does the school have a press officer? If not discuss with the senior team and governors the appointment of one.

3 When the right time comes, ask the parents for their views on the school using a suitable questionnaire. There are plenty available in many published texts with the Ofsted one being a simple way to start. When is the right time? This might be immediately you take up post, but it is more likely to be between one and three years into the job, because parents will have had a chance to assess the impact of the changes that will have occurred since you arrived.

Your parents are your best customers so listen to them, respond to their concerns and make sure you keep them informed. Also make sure that they understand what you and the school are trying to achieve.

The role of a press officer is important since it enables the school to keep its public profile high and positive. If there are regular press releases to the local newspaper by one person then a good rapport will build up and this is extremely valuable when incidents occur that could be reported negatively. The reporter will usually contact the school first before publishing if there is a good relationship and will be more inclined to listen to the school's version of events and then print a more positive story.

Working with business

Since 85 per cent of businesses employ fewer than ten people your school is a significant business in your community. As you gain more control of your own delegated budget and more capability to generate your own income then you become increasingly similar to the managing director or chief executive of a small to medium-sized business. So you should be spending time with these people by becoming an active member of your local Chamber of Commerce, a member of the Institute of Directors or a member of the Institute of Management. Find out what the needs of local business are and what your school's strengths are. Over time it will be possible to develop some types of support for the business community – probably in the area of staff training or use of the school's resources – that may make a significant contribution to your budget. As we have said elsewhere, with the development of a knowledge economy the skills and expertise within a school have an increasing value in a market economy. We need to find ways to exploit them.

Other agencies

Developing the perspective from earlier in the chapter about the probable new role of local government, there is some evidence to show that social services, library services and health services are being increasingly joined together to give a 'one stop shop' approach. Some of the joined-up services are being centred in schools so that the 'cradle to grave' support for individuals and families can centre around one location within the community.

TASK 52

Boundary spanning

Find out what the situation is in your area with regard to these services. In conjunction with your governors and senior staff consider if and how your school might work with these agencies to reduce barriers and bureaucracy. If you have an annual planning day with governors this would make a suitable topic for discussion, with the leaders of these agencies invited to participate.

Summary

Our intention is that, at the end of this chapter, you will have:

- understood the increasing importance of the community role of the schools

- realised that the relationship with LEAs is changing, as are their functions

- become aware that collaborative competition between schools in your locality is far more productive than isolationism or destructive competition

- learnt that communication and links with parents are changing as the nature of work changes for them and the way in which we can communicate with them also changes
- recognised that the links and relationships with business have become closer and more two-way in nature: schools have as much to sell to business as business sells to schools
- understood that the boundary spanning of government services is beginning to happen which is creating 'one stop shop' arrangements in communities for State support, including education.

Managing the workload

Introduction

There are always 20 things more you could do when you are Head. You have to find a way of stopping and focusing on the things that matter to you and on the space between. This chapter suggests ways of managing the four areas of life that interact: the job, personal professional development, family and relaxation.

Recognise the tasks

Work comes in many guises and how we respond to each gives us important clues as to how we can keep a sense of proportion in our lives.

There are:

- important issues to resolve
- urgent issues to deal with
- conversations
- observations
- regular duties to perform
- regular administration tasks to complete, daily and weekly
- interesting issues
- data analysis
- trivial matters
- and meetings … to chair, to participate in and to attend.

There are many ways of dealing with each type of activity and as much as possible we need to be aware of how we tackle each type of activity and try to keep a balance:

- immediate decision and action
- decide not to decide yet, perhaps get more information
- be reactive
- be proactive

- delegate

- monitor

- review

- reflect.

We operate as Heads at work by gaining information from as many sources as we can during the day. As each new bit of information is received we try to make sense of it and fit it into the picture we have of our organisation. We ask ourselves questions: Does this piece of data make a difference? How much does that person's view matter? Should we take any notice of this opinion? Does this data alter our perspective of our vision and so on. Sometimes this process is subconscious, sometimes more obvious, but it always happens. The difference for the Head is that we are responsible for all the answers. We can't think 'I can't be bothered', or 'Oh, that is someone else's responsibility'. For even when it is, we have a duty to inform that person whoever it may be.

After making decisions or receiving important information, the decision or information and its impact have to be communicated effectively to the right people at the right time and at the right place. The importance of effective communication cannot be overstated. As a Head you are standing at the top of the mountain and you can see further than most of those around you. So what seems clear and obvious to you can be unclear even to your senior deputy, and entirely meaningless to classroom teachers. Worse still, and more frequently than we ever imagine, is that the classroom teachers will interpret what is said in exactly the opposite way to what was intended. This can result in the opposite action happening or nothing at all or utter confusion.

Even when the decision or action is delegated to the right person, we have to monitor the process. Again, that person may have gained a different view of what is required and start the process going in the opposite direction to that intended.

—————— Become a plate spinner ——————

But how do you juggle all these competing tasks? One analogy of the role of the Head is that of the plate spinner. We have all seen one balancing spinning plates on sticks. He or she sets up more and more and we cannot believe just how many he or she manages to set up and keep going. As a Head we have to help get the plates spinning and we have to be able to see them all spinning and make sure none are about to stop and come crashing to the floor. If they are getting wobbly we have to intervene in some way and get them spinning properly again. We will, from time to time, stop one because it is no longer spinning in the right way or it no longer has value or relevance. It is usually better to stop the plate than just let it fall to the floor because, as we know, it will smash and then there will be an awful mess to clear up. This will take a great deal of unnecessary time, of which you have precious little to spare.

The analogy is not perfect, but it is one that has served many Heads well in helping to maintain a balance between all the competing pressures on them.

Time management

TASK 53

Diary analysis

Analyse your diary for the last month to find out how you spent your time. It can be laid out in a chart and a possible format is suggested in Table 17.1 below, although you may wish to ask your PA to set it up and keep it for you!

TABLE 17.1 Work chart

Engagement/activity	Number of people involved	Total time used	Unproductive time	Outcome – how effective was the time used?
Senior team meeting				
Planning Y10 options				
Governors' meeting, including preparation				
Dealing with the post, faxes and e-mail				
Reflection on the day				
…				

Charts like this can also be drawn up for other areas of life.

Time is 'lost' in a number of ways:

- allowing meetings to go on too long
- spending too much time on trivial matters to avoid facing difficult situations

- allowing conversations and telephone calls to meander, before or after the key points have been discussed

- having an untidy desk

- jumping from one item to another without dealing with the first issue properly

- having a poor filing system, particularly today a poor computer filing system because, like Topsy, it has 'just growed'

- lack of focus.

Apart from the three main types of work as a Head, leadership, management and administration, there are all the different people who want access to you. There are also the people you want access to and those whom you want kept from you as their demands are trivial and are more sensibly handled by a deputy, your PA or another member of staff. The demands on your time when you are a Head increase considerably and can easily get out of hand. In order to prevent this turning into overbearing pressure, either personally or by allowing too many people to expect to have too much access to you, it is crucial that you learn to prioritise both your personal time and your school as an organisation.

Understanding the difference between important and urgent tasks is easy, but living the difference in priorities is much more difficult. It also requires becoming as proactive as possible so that when the urgent overtakes the important it can be dealt with, without causing anyone unnecessary stress. For example, teachers as a body of people have become a reactive profession: Miss Jones storming into your office with an unruly student demanding action will immediately, and almost always, take precedence over a request from the local authority for next year's budget to be in by the end of the day. We are not saying that you should not always choose to respond to Miss Jones' demand, but that you need to put it into perspective and allocate enough time only to helping her or finding your deputy to deal with the matter. When dealing with people it frequently seems wise *at the time* to respond to the urgent demand.

With the changing role of the Head, we are increasingly acting as chief executives and there is a much greater need to spend far more of our time considering leadership issues, that is, being proactive. In fact, since schools are likely to become more independent in the future and not less, the need for proactive management and leadership, as we have said elsewhere, is going to increase.

As we all know, we have to be able to distinguish the *important* from the *urgent*. We think we know how to do this but how easy it is for the urgent to overtake the important and for the Head as 'crisis manager' or 'superman/woman' to take over. We seem to see ourselves as Horatius holding the bridge against the Etruscans, and easily slip into the role – there is more immediate response and adrenaline rush as we are helping to solve a crisis, which gives us a sense of satisfaction and gratification. This also helps us avoid that pile of tedious paperwork.

Some organisational hints that may help you get through the workload more quickly and enable you to have more time at your disposal are as follows:

- visit each task as few times as possible; once only should be the target
- learn to use technology effectively
- limit parent interviews and one-to-one meetings with staff to 30 minutes or less whenever possible, but always be sensitive to the situation
- keep lists to check off every day: however good your memory the number and range of tasks and activities that fall into your lap every day is too great to remember
- clear the desk as completely as possible each day and put remaining tasks in priority order for the next day
- keep to your schedule as much as possible. A good PA or secretary is invaluable, encourage him or her to help you achieve this
- develop the capacity to switch off from the job at the end of each day and for as much as possible at the weekend. Failure to be able to do this effectively will make the job immeasurably more stressful and will lead to poorer performance at work and a more difficult home life
- learn to delegate effectively, but do not abdicate responsibility
- try not to interfere, most staff want to do their jobs well and if they are given the space, more often than not they do
- give lashings of praise to staff and students, but make sure that the recipient is worthy of it. Praising mediocrity reduces standards very quickly. Recognise effort, criticise mediocrity and reward excellence
- be decisive, procrastination really is the thief of time
- don't write a paragraph when a sentence will do
- don't speak for ten minutes when one will do
- stick to your guns, know where you are going and make it clear to everyone. This will reduce the number of frivolous calls on your time
- keep your senior team enthusiastic. Their ability to transform the vision into reality is critical
- take part in a totally relaxing activity that is nothing to do with the job at least three times a week
- keep your sense of humour.

——————— Summary ———————

Our intention is that, at the end of this chapter, you will have:

- understood the importance of keeping the different parts of your life separate and balanced
- learnt that it is necessary to shut off work when you are relaxing by taking part in an all-absorbing activity
- realised that working closely with your secretary or PA to manage your diary and your time as rigorously as possible is a great time saver
- recognised that keeping the meetings you control as short as possible is prudent
- analysed your time and found out ways to save some of the 'wastage'
- seen the value in keeping your sense of humour and sense of fun.

—————————————————————

Future perspectives

Introduction

After you have been in post for three to five years you will find that you want to revisit some of your earlier decisions and ideas. The changes that you implemented in the honeymoon period at the beginning of your tenure have made their impact. The school is no longer the place it was. The new technology is being well used and is starting to need replacement. You are getting restless. The school is going along steadily but the imperative to make further change is pressing as others are improving faster than your school. Is the school starting to coast? It is time to revisit some of your original assumptions.

Reproduced here are two papers that were produced in the Spring and Summer 2000. One comes from a group of Heads and staff that belong to Vision 2020 – an action-focused think-tank. The second was produced by Liz Allen for the Local Government Association. Vision 2020 consists of mostly Heads and staff of specialist schools who have had the opportunity to see the effects of technology on learning and the many other changes that are discussed in this book. The papers provide food for further thought and will perhaps help you to launch your school into that paradigm shift that is required by all schools at some point in the next few years, if all the main thinkers and academics in this area are to be believed.

When we are looking forward we only ever see incremental change; we only notice that a paradigm shift has occurred when we look back. It is a real case of hindsight having perfect vision.

The first paper came from a Vision 2020 conference held over three days during the Spring and early Summer of 2000. Vision 2020 is a loose group of schools that consider futures thinking and action plans to get there. The strength of the group lies in the support for change within the group and the support of a number of highly regarded educational and change thinkers from around the world. The document involved contributions from about 100 schools and has been published by the Technology Colleges Trust to all its affiliated schools.

Circulate these texts among your senior staff and governors and discuss how some of the ideas might change your organisation in the next ten years. As the document suggests, take the ideas contained here and incorporate them in your next development plan. Many of them exist in some form in schools in this country or around the world.

The second document reproduced here with the kind permission of the author, Liz Allen, was recently published at the behest of the Local Education Authorities who had commissioned research into possible future roles and structures of local government.

A third document, recently published also on future perspectives is well worth reading to help you create your future vision. It is *Surviving the Future: Changing Education in a Changing World* by Trevor Kerry.

They are for you to read and hopefully will influence your thinking, planning and actions over the next few years.

——— Vision 2020 Development Plan ———
One World One School

Vision 2020 Conference Paper – July 2000

Foreword

This is a working paper. The V2020 Executive declared their intention to publish a document containing strategic plans and operational targets for school development over the next three years. This will form the basis of the development of the TC Trust's plans for educational thinking and for support of its schools over the period. In order to articulate a common vision, the ideas and priorities of member schools will be needed.

Consensus thinking is our aim, but we are realistic enough to recognise that a 'one size fits all' approach will not be appropriate. In formulating any action plan, therefore, the Executive will borrow the approach of our Australian colleagues[1] and prioritise on the 80%/20% rule – acknowledging that there will always be a proportion of schools for whom a particular idea or target will not be palatable.

After three separate days of presentations, discussions and visits to schools, this development plan has emerged. Over 100 schools affiliated to the TC Trust have been involved in its preparation. The authorship of the document is accredited to all of the participants during our three days of activities.

Please add to, comment on, or raise questions about any of them through the response mechanism given at the end of this paper.

Please also feel free to adopt any of the thinking, plans and targets and incorporate them into your own development or business plan, in fact we actively encourage this.

Within all our work, we have assumed mastery of the fundamentals of any successful school and that is: good behaviour, high standards and high expectations and the relentless pursuit of improvement.

—————— Executive Summary ——————

The structure of the plan is based on the work of Brent Davies and Linda Ellison as detailed in *Strategic Direction and Development of the School*. The content is based on the work of Brian Caldwell in *Scenarios for Leadership and Abandonment in the Transformation of Schools*.

The underpinning factors running through the work include a belief that if we are to build world class schools for a knowledge society then it is not sufficient merely to tinker with existing structures. A paradigm shift is required which puts the responsibility for driving schools forward firmly in the hands of school leaders and their communities and the responsibility for learning firmly in the hands of our students. It also involves radical re-thinking of what a school is, where it is located and what it does. Hence our discussions on school leadership, governance, pedagogy and creativity.

The paper suggests ideas and strategies for bringing about the cultural changes that will lead to this paradigm shift in the short, medium and long term.

---

1   *Education 2010 – A Preferred Future for Victorian Education*, published by the Victorian Association of State Secondary Principles, August 1996.

_____ Introduction _____

> 'Until one is committed, there is hesitancy, the chance to draw back, always ineffectiveness. Concerning all acts of initiative, there is one elementary truth the ignorance of which kills countless ideas and splendid plans: that the moment one definitely commits oneself, then Providence moves too ... Whatever you can do or dream, you can, begin it. Boldness has genius, power and magic in it. Begin it now.'

Goethe's words have resonance with the Vision 2020 group, which frequently cites the mantra 'Lead or get out of the way!'

Vision 2020 is a forum for futures thinking and development. Its distinguishing characteristic is that it is *not a forum for talking but for doing*. The project first saw the light of day at the St Ermin's Hotel, London, on 20 September 1996. It was a child of the first *HeadNet* project (*an earlier initiative which introduced 250 headteachers to e-mail and the Internet through hands-on workshops*). Thirty head-teachers, together with representatives from the ICT industry and academia, met to brainstorm the future of schooling. Since 1996, a number of workshops, seminars and conferences have been held, always with the focus of sharing innovative and radical ideas, often speculative but always pragmatic. In addition, the schools involved engaged in increasingly active networking via electronic media.

In 1997, a journal[2] was published to coincide with the first International V2020 Invitation Conference which was attended by delegates from Australia, Canada, and the USA. This event, in addition to indirectly bringing about two virtual EAZs, gave rise to a follow-up seminar in Melbourne in 1999, during a V2020 project study tour, and the second international conference which began on 4 May 2000 in London. This paper seeks to bring together the ideas and responses from that first stage of the conference and to move towards action planning for an education future in the UK. The key aim is to establish a vision of how teaching and learning should be organised in the 21st century, and to encourage stakeholder participation in realising that vision.

Up until now many of the changes that have occurred in secondary school education have been innovative and have helped drive up standards but they have not changed the fundamental nature of schools and their relationships to their students, parents and the wider community. In the meantime, the world in which these schools exist is changing radically, as the new economy begins a process of

---

2 Ibid.

transforming not just jobs but lifestyles and communities. This has been characterised by Tom Bentley of Demos into two opposing value sets which increasingly separate school from society.

He defines schools as hierarchical, standardised, information sparse, based on knowledge transmission and centralised control. They are also vertically integrated (divided into subject departments is the main curriculum logic) and custodial in nature. This is contrasted with the wider environment to becoming increasingly complex, unpredictable, network based, horizontally integrated and increasingly information rich. He also sees this world as changing rapidly and increasingly out of control. We do not believe that the school of the future should be unpredictable and out of control! This is not the kind of environment we would want for our children. On the other hand we do have a social responsibility to prepare young people for a world that is increasingly complex and information rich. The challenge, therefore, is to move schools towards the new model of society without destroying the values and ethos that are successful today.

In order to achieve this, we need to do more than tinker at the edges of school structures, i.e. changing the timetable, making learning more interactive and interesting, offering limited opportunities to develop independent learning skills and so on. We are really talking about a paradigm shift in terms of what makes a school and what its relationship is with its community. Some of these ideas will be addressed in this publication but include a radical re-think on school governance, curriculum and creativity.

The 2nd International Conference – Part I, 4 May 2000

'One World One School' is the theme of the Year 2000 V2020 three-part conference. Tom Bentley in his 'Learning Futures' project, outlined the national context, major trends and issues which faced arbiters of change and development. He contrasted the 20th century function of schools (to teach knowledge) with the 21st century need (to teach how to learn), and pointed out that schools are among the last set of institutions which have managed to resist fundamental organisational change. Describing the education sector response to environmental challenge as 'merely working the existing infrastructure harder', he pointed to the critical need for a deeper level of response to and acknowledgement of the new age in which:

– learning is embedded in all organisations (not just schools)

– there is a growing detachment from public systems

– new providers exist – virtual, corporate, value driven

– new forms of knowledge creation exist

– there is an increasing polarisation of access and opportunity.

Nigel Paine, CEO of the Technology Colleges Trust, summarised the trends in British Education today and the importance of futures thinking to help move education forward for tomorrow. He predicted that sharing knowledge electronically would be one of the key ways in which schools will learn from each other and from broader society. The only way that excellence will be encouraged and supported will be based on the development of internal mechanisms to sustain change rather than imposed criteria from external agents.

As the affiliated network of schools in the Technology Colleges Trust has demonstrated, the driving force for innovation rests within the school and the role of the Trust is increasingly to support, encourage and disseminate the innovation process.

Contributions from our International speakers, Professor Brian Caldwell[3] from Melbourne and Tom Upchurch from Atlanta, USA, focused the conference on the global commonality of the imperative for change, the potential barriers and some possible frameworks for planning. A common message was that 'stopping doing some things is one of the pre-functions of doing things differently'.

Experiential evidence of current developmental work was provided by David Crossley, former Principal of Jerudong International School, Brunei, and Merril Haeusler from Melbourne who steered us through the lessons learned via the Victorian Navigator Schools[4] programme. David shared with the conference the trials and tribulations of trying to set up a school for the future whilst holding on to a semblance of stability. Having adopted a UK curriculum for his students who came from 30 different countries and experienced a high level of education disruption through international mobility, his vision was their becoming part of a global classroom in which they could create, combine, collaborate, discuss, interact, learn, publish, research and share – a new pedagogy based on Information Communication & Collaboration Technology (ICCT).

Brian Caldwell identified nine separate domains of innovation. His premise was that 'Leadership in transformation and abandonment' has to be shown in all of them. Using the nine domains, V2020 members hosted response groups with a remit to address the concept of 'abandonment' which Brian had outlined. It was considered that this would provide a useful framework, but should not be viewed as a straitjacket.

3   *Scenarios for Leadership and Abandonment in the Transformation of Schools*, presented as keynote address at the 13th International Congress for School Effectiveness and Improvement, January 2000.

4   *Re-thinking Learning & Teaching – The Navigator Schools' Experience*, Report 1 – July 1998.

The Nine Domains of Innovation

- Innovation in Curriculum
- Innovation in Pedagogy
- Innovation in Design
- Innovation in Professionalism
- Innovation in Funding
- Innovation in Leadership
- Innovation in Management
- Innovation in Governance
- Innovation in Boundary Spanning

In each area not only are new ideas, structures and plans required but so too are ideas for abandonment for we cannot just pile one new structure or policy on top of another; we have to decide what we no longer need and plan systematically to remove it.

The next five years

The purpose of our recent deliberations has been to suggest actions, strategies and directions in which schools can develop over the next 18 months to five years. These suggestions are designed to fit in with the development of specialist schools in the UK and with the increasing globalisation of education and other aspects of life. The aim is to ensure that the UK has sufficient world class schools to enable enough young people to graduate in order to compete successfully in the global economy in our knowledge society. The challenge has never been greater and the competition has never been fiercer.

To some extent, many of the ideas put forward in V2020 conferences are already in place in some schools. The challenge is to encourage all schools to seek to re-design themselves, balancing systematic innovation with systematic abandonment.

Futures Thinking

The concept of Futures Thinking has been developed by Brent Davies and is explained in some detail in his book with Linda Ellison *Strategic Direction and*

Development of the School.[5] Its purpose is to pose the statements of where you want to be in ten to 20 years' time. The Vision 2020 conference paper *Our Vision* published in November 1999, described scenarios based on a 'wish list' of education futures and some of the statements about school that have been culled from various sources would suggest that, if we get the development right, learning for young people growing up might have some of the following characteristics and facets:

■ schools will be part of learning networks or communities

■ the boundaries between types and age ranges of schools will not exist

■ between five and 20 present day schools will form a Learning Community or Network

■ schools that are part-private/part-state funded

■ the best Learning Networks will be part of a global group of World Class 'Schools'

■ the home will be an extension of the Learning Network and many other networks to which the family will choose to belong

■ all students will have Individual Education Plans and, from the age of 14, considerable control of their own learning

■ universities will remain core institutions in the development of knowledge and all learning communities will be linked directly to at least one

■ the Learning Network will be the main provider of training to the business community and will have an active entrepreneurial section that sells the services to the local, national and international community

■ the Learning Network will enable its information network to manage the learning needs of all in its community and it will provide access to the worldwide links necessary for a world class community

■ the adults who work in the community will be teachers, para-teaching professionals, business people working part time and other adults taking a break from other work in which they are involved

■ the best teachers will be able to sell their services to many learning communities around the globe either directly or digitally. There will be a group of highly paid highly respected expert teachers and presenters who will have a worldwide profile

---

5   *Strategic Direction and Development of the School*, Brent Davies and Linda Ellison, published by Routledge, 1999

- students will attend school by negotiation from age 14 to fit in with the other demands society will place on young people. The culture of the teenager will diminish

- teacher training will involve the study of neuro-science, cognitive psychology, emotional intelligence and creativity, as well as a detailed study of the learning and teaching styles of each individual teacher. A special study of thinking skills and learning how to learn will also be important parts of the training

- the concept of the school day and term will disappear

- the use of technology as both a management tool for the teacher and a delivery mechanism for learning will be ubiquitous, fuelled by developments such as the electronic book and wireless technologies allowing constant networking, regardless of location

———— Innovation and Abandonment ————

Part 1 Conference Response

What follows is a distillation of the group discussions, e-mail correspondence, and additional contributions provided by delegates following the first day of this three-part conference. The information is presented here as a working document for completion, amendment and supplementation.

Domain 1: Innovation in Curriculum

In the year 2000, we face an exciting yet challenging goal, to create a *curriculum for the future* that prepares young people for future learning and future employment in a market place where the context will demand greater flexibility, adaptability, responsibility and imagination. We accept the Demos CreativeNet target of reducing content in the National Curriculum by 30 per cent within ten years and replacing that with a creative curriculum that develops process skills such as thinking, analysing, problem solving and team working.

The curriculum that operates in the year 2000 shows increasing flexibility, especially at Key Stage 4. Pupils heading for Key Stage 4 in September 2000 already have the scope to be disapplied from certain areas of the curriculum in order to specialise in key areas or to reinforce their learning and skills in others. Our vision for the future will see pupils *negotiating with their learning mentors* over the curriculum they follow. This may contain a balance between the core content that educational leaders at national, local and school levels regard as appropriate whilst the remainder of the time pupils negotiate over the areas they want to specialise in. These may include subjects that pupils anticipate following in more detail at Key Stage 5 or Higher Education, or because a personal skills set in one curriculum area demands increased access. The Arts, Sport, Modern Languages could all become increasingly important when this becomes the norm.

The flexible curriculum model also points the way towards developing truly *autonomous learners*. Pupils for part of their curriculum time may work on-line, accessing learning tasks or entire courses from the World Wide Web, providing schools with the flexibility over teacher allocation time. Does a group of pupils working electronically in this way need to be 'taught' or 'facilitated'? Schools will increasingly be looking to create a 'virtual' curriculum to operate alongside their 'live' mode of operation. Pupils will exploit the sophisticated processes of *wireless technology* to access 'anytime anywhere' learning. The electronic collaboration between schools, teachers, pupils and classrooms will reinforce the culture of the family of schools.

School Intranets, made available for other schools to contribute to and draw from, will contain materials from lessons, extension tasks, links to key sites, and the assessment methodology linked to that piece of work. When this vision is a reality for the critical mass of schools, we begin to free teachers from the log jam of marking and preparation, freeing them to *focus upon the styles of learning* and the pedagogical processes that fundamentally underpin good teaching.

The design of the curriculum must be forward looking. A *flexible school day* will offer pupils the chance to maximise their learning time beyond the traditional six hour day, within and beyond the timetabled programme. Lessons will be longer as schools move towards the 'two period' day where pupils spend half day sessions in curriculum areas, tuning in to the learning processes demanded by each subject without having to interrupt a learning experience that is gathering momentum simply because the school bell rings.

Curriculum teams will consider what the most appropriate style of delivery will be. Introductory lessons for large cohorts of pupils balanced with tutorial sessions moves planning away from the assumption that all learning takes place in units of 30 pupils. The extended learning day will provide schools with further opportunities to facilitate community learning networks, putting into practice meaningful Lifelong Learning *programmes for pupils and their families.*

Future curriculum planners will remove the distinction between academic and vocational education. Links with the e-commerce world will become established as a fundamental entitlement for all pupils. High level, industry and business based vocational courses will begin at 14 and extend to 19 years old and beyond. Pupils will compete with each other for the degree sponsorship that will address the work place demands of industrial sponsors.

Schools will begin to adjust from the concept of year long curriculum models and plan in whole key stages. *Modular learning frameworks* will create the demand for movement from the traditional three-term year towards the five-term model where each eight-week module is assessed and reported to parents. Teachers will continue to work in teams to plan the curriculum that they believe meets the learning needs of groups and individuals. The challenge for school leaders is to ensure that a team based approach reaps rewards for teachers in terms of efficiency and workload, and that their access to learning technologies avoids duplication and ensures that the digital workload replaces paper based tasks.

Summary	
Abandon	Innovate by
School bells	Use watches
30 per cent of National Curriculum	30 per cent creative curriculum
Fixed days	Variable days
Fixed lesson times	Variable lesson times
	Extend day
Fixed year	Fixed points in the year
	Online access 24 hours a day

Domain 2: Innovation in Pedagogy

Research into the new pedagogy emerging from the ICT revolution is not yet rooted in the consciousness of the profession or in the institutions which train new teachers, although the work of universities such as Anglia University's Ultralab (Dr Stephen Hepple) on inter-active multi-media learning approaches indicates the crucial changes which will be required in response to new learning media.

A focus on existing practice generated the following possible alternatives.

Existing practice to be abandoned	Alternative approaches to trial
Teaching strategies which do not address the learning needs of disaffected students	Teach key skills through work-related learning programmes
Teaching strategies which do not enable sophisticated learners to gain challenging learning experiences	Disapply the timetable for gifted students in favour of individual learning programmes with tutorial support
One lesson fits all	Team working and planning, IEPs for all
Teaching strategies which do not support transfer of learning: skills v content	Focus on thinking skills, literacy and numeracy strategies
Marking, grading and other assessment practices (GCSE) which do not support learning; assignments to students which occupy time rather than enhance learning	New assessment practices which inform learning
The isolation of teachers from each other in developing good practice; meetings which do not support pedagogy	Build master practitioner groups with a focus on publishing teacher developed learning resources
Fewer teachers as founts of all knowledge	More teacher as learning managers: teacher as 'superstar'?
Teacher restricted to classroom	Teacher available to all through technology
Timetable structures which do not enable teachers to plan learning	Timetables which structure in collaborative development time
The use of ICT in situations where there is no learning gain	Collaborative development ICT applications in the curriculum
KS4 teaching styles at post-16	A higher education teaching style
The principle of a two-year KS4 course	Develop a modular curriculum which addresses the differing needs of pupils as they progress through KS4

Domain 3: Innovation in Design

- We are more concerned with *designing a school*, not a school building. Online learning opportunities available to children in the future may serve to move away from the concept of 'school' as we now know it.

- External factors – parents, the wider community, employers, government views – will have an impact on any shaping of schools of the future by teachers.

- The *National Curriculum would have to change* to allow for changes in the organisation of schools.

- We couldn't abandon children to a virtual experience. *In loco-parentis issues* would have implications for the future design of schools and how children progressed.

- We have the facility for focusing much more on individual needs. Whilst we might not in the future have school buildings as we have now, we would still value the idea of children coming together for *social purposes*.

- We should focus on *individualised needs* regardless of age. Children need to be shown how to learn and the opportunities available to let them do what is best for them in their own individual way.

- People *networking* help each other; we can pick up so much information from other people so children will need to have contact and interact with each other.

- It has to be remembered that in future access to education will be *a 24 hour operation*.

Summary

Abandon	Innovate by
Four walls of the classroom	Online classrooms
Four walls of the school	Online schools
Existing classroom structures	Re-designing learning environments to reflect teamwork and access to technology

Domain 4: Innovation in Professionalism

Three issues that look set to dominate teaching over the coming decades are *recruitment, retention and development*. Recruitment and retention are proving much harder in an economy that is enjoying continual expansion. The deployment of business models within the public sector and the highly public demonisation of this area have led to a decline in the concept of public service. Underlying this problem has been a lack of capital investment, which only serves to widen the gulf between the worlds of business and education. Demographic changes make the related recruitment problems worse as education must now compete within a diminishing labour market.

Solving these difficulties will not be easy. Failing to solve them will result in education at all levels coming to a precipitous halt. Doubtless machine driven approaches to learning will develop rapidly but without *teachers or learning managers* mapping this process there will be significant problems. Three suggestions for the way forward.

First, we need to *invest in the capital infrastructure* of our schools. We need to construct modern institutions that are purpose-built. The current replacement rate for schools in the UK using PFI (Private Finance Initiative) approaches is something in the order of 4000 years. We need a route that is faster and more cost effective.

Second we must ensure that government back away from constant intervention in education and instead set broad targets that allow schools flexibility in achieving them. Much of this is about reducing bureaucracy and simplifying systems. *Equally however it is about establishing a clear long-term vision and communicating this effectively.*

Third reform of the education system needs to be *teacher-led*. We need to involve teachers as professionals and celebrate their achievements. The presentation of teachers' views needs to come less from general secretaries of trades unions and more from the likes of the General Teaching Council.

None of this will be easy but unless as a nation we are able to get the political contexts of our schools positively depicted we are unlikely to attract, retain and develop professionals to staff our schools. This is the challenge to which we must respond.

Summary	
Abandon	Innovate by
The concept of full-time, graduate recruitment to teaching	Part-time portfolio teachers; mid-career change teachers; short term and fixed contracts for those intending to return to industry
One year university based teacher training	Flexible school based teacher training
Of historical attitudes	Development of a new professionalism

Domain 5: Innovation in Funding

As school leaders we are all working in a time of transition in the funding of state education. In the UK developments in curriculum and in raising achievement have been shown to occur best where schools are in charge of their own budgets and when they are funded directly against set targets. The specialist schools in the UK have to raise sponsorship and then have a fixed term targeted plan. In exchange for this they are given extra funding by the government based on number of pupils. The funding may be withdrawn if targets are not met. This is a relatively new way of encouraging educational development but the outcome shows that it works: standards are being raised at twice the national average. (Jesson)

Specialist schools have become used to raising other extra funds, especially in relation to providing for access to the new technologies for their students. This *combination of a basic provision from the State and new partnerships with businesses and other agencies* points the way for future funding solutions. The problem at the moment is that it is much easier for some schools, because of their geographical position or their size, to attract the extra funding. Although being part of a bidding culture may be satisfying when the bid is successful, more and more developments seem to have to rely on bids, so that in some large schools one or more members of the senior management team are constantly involved in paperwork, preparing or evaluating bids. Some educational institutions employ full-time bid writers.

Tom Bentley has written of 'releasing ourselves from over-dependence on taxation and public spending...filtered through an expensive and slow-moving bureaucratic system'. Creative solutions to funding innovation are necessary.

These will come about as more and more schools move away from being a service provided by a local education authority to being hubs of the life of their communities. There is a need for 'joined-up solutions to joined-up problems' as Brian Caldwell has stated; we should be looking, for example, at the possibilities of the full-service schools in the USA, where all local resources are placed on one site. We should also be examining the exciting possibilities of the local specialist school being the learning hub for the wider community. The school has the technical resources to link homes and schools to the broadband area learning network, making cost-effective use of the investment in learning technologies and providing 24 hour access. Schools need greater investment to be able to provide suitable education for young people for the knowledge society. This investment must come from the public purse but can also come from many private sponsors who have a vested interest in the success of lifelong education. But both public and private investors are rightly looking for a cost-effective return for their cash. Inevitably more and more of the funding of schools will be linked with outcome.

The political concept of 'free education for all' has muddied the waters of parental contributions. Schools in this country are often reluctant to ask parents directly for help in expanding educational provision for their children. They are forced into cloaking such a request in various guises such as raffles, dances and car boot sales where the teachers are the principal fund-raisers as well as employees of an under-resourced provision. Brian Caldwell asks whether there is a place 'for a parent contribution, either covenanted or mandated, in cash or kind?' In relation to the possibility of one-to-one access to the new technologies Microsoft have recently come up with a format (*the E-Learning Foundation*) for covenanting to a trust fund where businesses and parents can gain tax relief by payments to a fund for such provision. This idea is catching on in individual schools, groups of schools and in whole education authorities. It points the way to a new way of funding the expensive resources that are now absolutely necessary for what is known as 'world class education'.

Education needs to look at the strategies that are used in the business world for developing new brands, for example, how is it that a small coffee shop in Seattle became a world-wide chain within ten years? Is it possible for educational establishments to develop a world-class brand that can be franchised?

Summary	
Abandon	Innovate by
Current funding arrangements	Increase percentage funding going to schools directly
Concept of 'State provides all'	Developing educational businesses
	Developing the concept of venture philanthropy

Domain 6: Innovation in Leadership

Most research into what makes a school successful returns to the simple fact that the quality of the leader determines, to a large extent, the ethos, the value systems and ultimately the success of the school.

Developing outstanding leaders is thus an essential part of the process of change. The culture that is considered normal for a school environment is one that is low risk. The nature of change now is such that it is becoming less risky implementing change than taking what has often been regarded as the safe option, namely maintaining the status quo. There is thus a need to develop a new breed of leader for our schools, which has been called by Peter Drucker a 'Change Leader'.

Change Leadership

Peter Drucker has written widely on management and leadership for over half a century and is one of the most widely respected professionals in this area. In his recent book, *Management Challenges for the 21st Century*, he identifies tomorrow's key issues for businesses – both in the private and public sector, including schools and universities – and the strategies and principles involved in meeting the challenges. However, the role of the leader of the organisation, he suggests, will become paramount as the pace of change continues to quicken. He suggests that those organisations which will survive and flourish have to have Change Leaders at the top. These are individuals who flourish on change – Peters would describe them as 'Thriving on Chaos' – and who actively seek to *make* the future. Somewhat depressingly he suggests that many of those who do take this approach will fail, but he also says that all of those who do NOT try *will even more certainly fail.*

'One thing is certain for developed countries – and probably for the entire world: we face long years of profound changes. The changes are not primarily economic changes. They are not even primarily technological changes. They are changes in demography, in politics, in society, in philosophy and, above all, in world-view ... It is futile to try to ignore the changes and to pretend that tomorrow will be like yesterday, only more so ... To try to make the future is highly risky. It is less risky, however, than not to try to make it.'

The implications are clear and these are some of the areas that are crucial pre-cursors to effecting changes in the way that education is provided:

- We have to find and articulate clearly the ethical and moral principles that form the basis for education and for our society.

- We will require leadership of the highest order that transcends headship and focuses on the advancement of learning.

- We need to accept that things don't have to be done the way they always have been done.

- We will require Heads with a clarity of vision and a clear understanding of the way things are now so that they can plan how to get from here to there.

- We will need Heads and school leaders who have the boldness and confidence to carry through their plans. They will also need confidence and steadfastness as the way will not be easy.

- We will need the National College for School Leadership to nurture these aspiring Heads. We will also need the College to provide the support and camaraderie the existing Heads will require to sustain them in their work.

- We require leaders who have the capacity to deliver high expectations and who have the capacity to bring all their community together to work in common purpose for its success.

Summary

Abandon	Innovate by
Ad hoc and random preparation for leadership	Structured preparation of future leaders at all levels in schools
Constraints on leadership	Developing teachers as leaders

Summary

Abandon	Innovate by
Lack of recognition	Focusing on the future, not just the present
Over reliance on the administrative function to justify the role	Developing change leaders
Over reliance on re-active leadership	Develop pro-active leadership
	Developing and facilitating entrepreneurial leaders

Domain 7: Innovation in Management

Management in the 21st Century should move from exclusive hierarchical structures to include all staff. Sharing management, values and vision, with students, parents, governors and the community should be the rule rather than the exception. Make all teachers leaders and managers and all students teachers!

Abandon	Innovate by
Old hierarchies	**Teams in school**
Often, those in power have a vested interest in the status quo because they made it so. Avoid exclusive management layers.	Look for the innovative and creative in teams and allow them to develop in management roles regardless of status; use younger staff's management skills.
Narrow approach to attainment	**Motivation of learners**
Schools largely assess through linguistic and mathematical means. Widen it out!	Learning styles and preferences Multiple intelligences Accelerated learning If we accept these principles for teaching and learning then why not for management.
Routine/tradition	**Develop creativity**
Habit is a deadener, tradition is slovenliness. 'You may have always done it that way but it doesn't work.'	And act using it.

Abandon	Innovate by
Business meetings	**Training and development meetings**
Abandon meetings which are not geared to outcomes.	The focus of meetings should be the planning and dissemination of effective teaching and learning and how to achieve it.
Paper	**Role of electronic communications**
Use a bulletin.	Exploit the possibilities of ICT in the management of learning.
Reactive	**Proactive**
Delegate	Strategic and operational planning. Predict the future and plan for it.
8:30 – 4:30	**Plan for life-long year-round community resource centres**

Domain 8: Innovation in Governance

Among the innovations in UK school governance over the past decade have been the CTC initiative, the grant-maintained movement, the specialist schools initiative, the Education Action Zones and, more recently, the Excellence in Cities and the City Academies proposals. All of these heralded new ways of governing schools and new forms of partnership. The devolution of funding and the involvement of business sponsors as governors were the most significant factors of change, bringing about a culture of market-led education and leading to increased efficiency of school management and a stronger sense of accountability.

In the USA, the growth of the Charter Schools movement and the rise of the 'schools for profit' sector, within which schools are operated by publicly quoted companies under contract, reflect a shift away from total public sector governance.

Alternative ownership and accountability of institutions may be needed to accommodate the variety of access and delivery mechanisms which Learning Networks or Communities would service.

How will this fit with a strongly held belief that State education should be entirely State funded?

Summary	
Abandon	Innovate by
Schools as islands	Schools taking over or amalgamating with other schools
Separate phase education	Networks of schools as communities under one governing body and cross phase
	Developing full service learning organisations
	Developing school brands
Existing educational support structures	New models of educational support selected by the school

Domain 9: Innovation in boundary spanning

Caldwell's review of this his 9th 'domain' is highly informative but not sufficiently radical. The emphasis is very much about *joined up thinking* across government departments and there is praise rightly for the government of Alberta's attempts in effect to merge the relevant departments and their budgets in order to make a difference.

A new approach for the specialist school movement is needed – one that gives individual schools and groups of schools or indeed other organisations (public or private) the right and the duty to cross boundaries locally to *span the fields of education, health and community*. This would amount to something called 'a total resource strategy' with the educators in the lead role in terms of empowering and leading local communities

Specialist school Heads would not only be responsible for new ways of learning through technology but would be expected to lead local *analyses of blockages to learning*. These would obviously involve a catalogue of the usual suspects; poverty, low expectations, health issues, socially fragile communities. The old analysis of such indicators being crippling without intervention from a host of other government directed and funded, and often competing, agencies would go. In its place would be a flexible locally directed and funded approach led by the specialist school educators. The funding would have one aim – the removal of blockages to learning in order to raise achievement, self esteem and confidence in local communities so that at last the playing field begins to level for all in a global employment market.

The specialist schools would become accountable for community progress measured by educational achievement and subsequent employability.

Total resource strategy means what it says; in local areas the fusing of education, health, social services, lottery and other funding with an education achievement focus.

There are elements of this in place already of course: EAZs, HAZs the new 'Connexions' service, the 'Excellence in Cities' programme. However, all of these lack really short and quick command chains and have, because of present inter departmental structures, diffuse systems of leadership. Specialist school Heads are by their nature comfortable with innovation and also with sharp accountability. Such leadership skills coupled with a wish to ensure raising of achievement makes them well placed to integrate and drive the other aspects of the social agenda.

Summary

Abandon	Innovate by
Single service provision	A total resource strategy
One track thinking	An holistic approach
Separate support centres	One-stop shop for the whole community

———— Strategic Planning ————

Strategic Planning links the immediate operation targets to the long-term vision. It is here that the 'domains of innovation' are most helpful. The strategic aims shown below are offered as stimulus for discussion.

TABLE 1 Strategic aims over 3–5 years

Domain	Innovation	Abandonment
Curriculum	■ First major examinations at 18 ■ New Creativity and Design courses ■ Neuroscience courses ■ Thinking Skills courses	■ Abolition of GCSEs ■ Significant reduction in NC

Domain	Innovation	Abandonment
Pedagogy	■ Teaching takes place in groups of 100 students ■ Tutorials take place in groups of 3 or 4 ■ Numbers of para-teachers equal teachers ■ All lessons available online ■ All assessment available online	■ Traditional classroom teaching in groups of 30
Design	■ New year and day structures implemented ■ New groupings of students in schools	■ Traditional day and year structures no longer exist ■ Tutor groups of 30 no longer exist
Professionalism	■ GTC sets and maintains professional standards ■ A new professional passion exists in some schools	■ Union approach disappears
Funding	■ Majority of revenue funding comes direct to schools ■ 20 per cent of revenue generated from business activity ■ Schools operate asset accounting processes	■ Current funding arrangements
Leadership	■ Heads have become Chief Executives ■ Qualifications for headship are mandatory ■ The Head is now often the leader of five or more schools	■ Groups of Heads (Chief Executive Officers) meet regularly to consider changes and what structures and activities can be abandoned.

Domain	Innovation	Abandonment
Management	■ School structures built around 'knowledge management' ■ Network management structures in place	■ Departmental structures in secondary schools disappear ■ Year group pastoral structures disappear
Governance	■ Schools able to amalgamate into large learning networks ■ Learning networks can be more easily established ■ New local government link to learning networks are being introduced	■ Current support to schools is radically reviewed ■ Current structure for support services
Boundary spanning	■ Some schools exist which contain the local health, police and social services functions within the one institution	■ Duplication of effort and resources reduced in these communities

———— Action Planning ————

Some plans that could, and perhaps should, be adopted by leading schools, specialist or otherwise, within the next 18 months to three years are suggested in Table 2 below.

It is intended that the list should have the following effects:

– be challenging (*but taking action is less risky than doing nothing*)

– provoke discussion within the learning institution (*so that some of the suggestions at least are incorporated in the next institutional Development Plan*).

– encourage groups of local Heads to join together, and meet regularly to effect changes that they have in common and to discuss other changes that are ripe for implementation.

TABLE 2 Operational targets within three years

Domain	Innovation	Abandonment
Curriculum	■ Introduction of streamlined National Curriculum ■ Introduction of new Post-16 courses and structure ■ Introduction of wide range of vocational courses at KS4 and Post-16 ■ Plan online course approach to learning ■ Introduce CISCO/Microsoft style industry courses	■ Cease to offer some traditional subjects
Pedagogy	■ Introduce whiteboard technology for teaching lead lessons ■ Introduce or develop 'Thinking Skills' courses or 'Learning to Learn' courses	
Design	■ Decide best learning time and structure and implement new day	■ Switch off bells ■ Abolish end of Year reports in favour of regular short assessment reports
Funding	■ Plan and begin implementation of income generating activities	
Professionalism	■ Work with your staff to look at professional standards and implement ■ Pass on these new standards to the GTC	

Domain	Innovation	Abandonment
Leadership	■ Reassess your vision ■ Aim for 'co-operative competition' ■ Start training your senior team and middle managers in leadership skills ■ Establish regular links with other groups of Heads both local and national ■ Establish a leadership consultancy with a group of like-minded Heads	■ Abandon fence sitting: be bold!
Management	■ Reassess your management structure ■ Realign to reflect new values and culture	■ Rigid hierarchical structures
Governance	■ Begin to examine ways of joining schools together with other like-minded schools	
Boundary spanning	■ Seek out and study those schools that have already integrated other local services under one roof and one management.	

Stepping stones to schools of the future

> *Life can be best understood backwards but you have to live it forwards!'*

In our hearts we know we should be looking to the future, uncertain though it is, and starting a process of backwards planning but so many pressures push us towards incremental change. League tables, examination results, the needs of the current generation of students all argue for safety first and all discourage innovation. Strategic thinkers like Drucker, Papert, Handy, Gerstner and others argue for nothing less than complete reengineering. However, the reality of our schools means that an approach that combines backwards planning by helping schools envision what might be combined with strategies that take schools forward from where they are now is likely to be the most effective.

We all know that schools or learning organisations of the future are going to be quite different from those of today. We all know how little schools have changed compared to so many other organisations. Charles Handy gives us some clues on how to proceed and some real challenges for us to respond to. The challenge he puts to us is to take charge of the future rather than simply respond to it. Yet he feels that we need to change the whole basis of our educational system: from one built on the implicit assumption that all the problems in the world have been solved and the teacher knows the answers, to one where the job of the teacher is to help students know what to do with the ever growing font of knowledge and how to do it. In his words:

> 'To make the future happen we need to be self confined and believe in our own worth. That's what schools should teach us'.

However for many of us within schools there are few surprises here and our schools are already at least beginning to have this sort of emphasis. We also know that the future will be more uncertain than the past. All of this suggests that we should take longer term decisions based on what we feel the future will hold but we should have the confidence to reverse some of those decisions and abandon them if they are wrong.

Providing opportunities to plan from then to now

High level ICT skills, project management and tomorrow's leadership and team work skills can all find their place and be accredited if we want. The space liberated throughout the curriculum in KS4 and by the more recent changes to the primary curriculum provides us with real opportunities. From this we can move to change today's curriculum into tomorrow's too. This is how we can plan from then to now.

We don't need to abandon the past all at once so we won't be abandoning our educational equivalent of the bottom-line – our examination results.

Some argue that we are going to see the end to schools, as we know. In looking to the future we should explore what this might mean and why. It is easy to criticise schools but I expect that they will exist at least within our lifetime. They provide a social as well as an academic function. There is a future for schools, but not the factory school of the current century that was designed to meet very different needs. Fundamentally learning is a social experience and schools are as a good a place as any for people to learn together. Technology should be the servant of the learner enabling us all in Peter Drucker's words, 'to do new things not just old things better.' The school's role becomes one where we give all learners both confidence and competence in the current and future use of technology and one where we enable them both to learn now and to manage their own learning throughout life.

Vision 2020 schools have a track record of implementing innovative change within their environments. Our objective now is to bring about the metamorphosis of the current system in order to meet the needs of the new century, through the exploitation of emerging technologies and new thinking about knowledge transmission. We believe that it is essential to focus on futures thinking and harness the collective knowledge, experience and influence of our network to produce a workable map for development planning in the next decade.

As a reader of this document, your views on this publication are very important. The idea behind it is not simply to read and absorb but to feed back to improve and update the document in a dynamic relationship between the TC Trust and schools.

———— V2020 Executive Group 2000 ————

The current Executive members are listed below. It is the intention of the TC Trust to expand the group to reflect the new regional structure of the network.

David Carter, David Crossley, Mike Gibbons, Frank Green, Howard Kelly (Australia), Pam Kemp, Keith Nancekievill, Nigel Paine, David Triggs, Ken Walsh

Extended Executive members: Chris Gerry, Keith McCorkindale

_____ Future models of local education _____

Introduction

The local education service has been in a state of almost permanent revolution over the last decade. With the National Curriculum and national tests, development planning at both school and LEA level which incorporates target setting, and a regime of external inspection and intervention, the best value performance management framework for raising school standards is already in place. Fair Funding gives schools greater autonomy and responsibility, yet other developments are drawing them into new forms of collaboration with other schools and with a wide range of public, private and voluntary sector partners. Education has a pivotal role to play in the Government's agenda for tackling deprivation and social exclusion. Sure Start and New Deal for Communities initiatives, Early Excellence Centres, Education and Health Action Zones all place schools at the heart of community governance; whilst plans for reform at 16+ and the new Learning and Skills Council, will realign school education with further education and the world of work.

Although local education authorities have, of necessity, had to change alongside the education reforms, statutory reforms to local government political structures and delivery systems are only now beginning to catch up and frame the local context in which self-managing schools can thrive. The duty of best value with its emphasis on continuous review and improvement of services, was introduced in April 2000. Its necessary 'companion' – the Local Government Organisation and Standards Bill which will introduce new ways of working – is currently making its way through Parliament.

The principal aim of this New Local Government Network project on Future Models of Local Education is to map the parallel developments in education and local government modernisation, look for the connections between them, and explore a series of 'futures' in local education structure and delivery. What will 'local education' mean in 2020? What systemic changes may be needed to funding regimes, for example, or school management structures, to support effective local education? And, crucially, where does local government need to focus its attention over the next decade so as to provide an effective lead for local people and their local schools?

—— Visions of the future: local schools ——

The first major education act of the new Labour government consolidated many aspects of the significant reforms introduced by successive Conservative governments in the 80s and 90s. Although the excesses of the free-market model have been trimmed, self-managing schools, operating within a strong national performance framework, are now a fixture of the English and Welsh educational landscapes.

But education reforms haven't ended with the latest education Act, and nor are they likely to as globalisation and the information age challenge and change society at an ever faster pace. Schools, as front line services, grapple with these changes on a daily basis: more mobile, more plural communities, changing value systems and loss of certainty. As learning institutions they have to try to make sense of them, help their pupils make sense of them and prepare their pupils for life in the knowledge society.

In his book, *Learning Beyond the Classroom*, Tom Bentley identifies three major challenges facing schools today. The first is the place of education in an information society. When 'information can be collected and synthesised and communicated with more speed, precision and power than we have ever known before', it challenges both the way we learn and our attitudes towards conventional schooling. Schools must help learners sift out and apply the information that is useful to them. Public education systems 'must not only provide good quality learning in themselves, but also full access to the knowledge resources offered elsewhere'. And as those resources and the technology are constantly developing, so teachers have to adapt and develop at a faster pace than ever before.

The second is about values. Education helps to 'glue society together', and in our increasingly plural age it becomes more, not less, important that schools help pupils to recognise what it is that binds us together. Education Acts conflate moral education with religious education and 'mainly Christian' acts of worship, but 'when value changes come from all directions, formed and shaped by complex fluid processes' the real challenge for schools is to link moral education more closely to civic education, so as to provide a common core of values shared by diverse communities.

The third major challenge is how education can compete with the 'dazzling array of distractions and alternative pursuits' that the information age has to offer young people, and motivate them to 'concentrate, work purposefully and learn for themselves?' Should schools continue to operate as holding institutes which educate students between the hours of nine and three, or are more flexible models of schooling needed for the future?

In its National grid for Learning Development Plan, Somerset LEA has listed the impact of ICT on seven key aspects of the work of the education service:

Aspect 1: ICT radically extends learning opportunities

Aspect 2: ICT is changing what must be learned

Aspect 3: ICT is providing alternative opportunities for where and when things are learned

Aspect 4: ICT is providing sophisticated ways to manage the learning process and to increase its effectiveness

Aspect 5: ICT is changing teaching practice

Aspect 6: ICT is revolutionising the management and administration of the education service

Aspect 7: ICT is increasing community involvement in the education process.

All these pressures demand a fundamental re-think on the nature and purpose of schools – a step-change from a model that David Hargreaves once described as 'a curious mix of the factory, the asylum and the prison', towards one where schools become centres of learning in their neighbourhoods, open 24 hours a day and responsive to learning on demand. Writing in 1994, David Hargreaves argued that we need to 'transform our schools and teachers to catch up with the mosaic world of institutional fluidity, multiple or portfolio work styles and highly distinctive sub-communities'. Only then can they become 'sources of satisfaction to those who teach and learn and so achieve the standards of excellence and performance levels so urgently needed' (*The Mosaic of Learning: Schools and Teachers for the Next Century*, Demos, 1994).

The government is responding to these challenges with a stream of new policy initiatives from Downing Street and the Department for Education and Employment, all with a relentless focus on raising achievement, and a willingness to explore new methods of delivery. Many of these developments have a resonance with changes to schools systems in other countries as they grapple with the same conundrums.

In their book Beyond the Self-Managing School, *Australian academics, Brian Caldwell and Jim Spinks, have charted the following 'Tracks for Change' as new school systems develop:*

'1. Centrally determined frameworks of goals, policies, priorities, curriculum, standards and accountabilities will be strengthened.

2. More authority, responsibility and accountability will be decentralised to schools.

3. There will be unrelenting pressure to achieve high levels of learning outcomes for all students.

4. Schools will play an important role in the knowledge society and advances in technology will be central in this effort.

5. There will be a high level of coherence across areas of the curriculum, schools as workplaces will be transformed, the existing fabric of schools will be rendered obsolete, and globalisation will be evident in learning and teaching.

6. A new concept of professionalism will emerge, based around necessary and unprecedently high levels of knowledge and skill.

7. A capacity to work in teams will be required in virtually every facet of professional practice.

8. Policies to address issues of access and equity will be required for the successful utilisation of information and communications technology.

9. Virtual schooling will be a reality in every setting, but there will always be a place called school.

10. A continually updated 10 year time horizon will be necessary for every school to plan the journey along these tracks for change.'

In his speech to the North of England Education Conference in January 2000, David Blunkett pulled the pieces of the education policy jigsaw together (*Raising Aspirations in the 21st Century*, January 2000). His speech is uncompromising about the need to raise educational standards and aspirations, and provides clear markers about the government's intentions for transforming education to build a 'world class education system'. The National Grid for Learning will link all schools up to the information superhighway, creating limitless possibilities for new professional networks, and speeding the development of new forms of teaching and learning. More targets and initiatives are being introduced to boost performance at transfer at KS3. Particular emphasis is being placed on initiatives that tackle social exclusion in a 'joined-up' way, linking education to wider regeneration initiatives. City Learning Centres with state of the art ICT facilities are being set up through the Excellence in Cities initiative that will offer extended hours learning opportunities for parents, pupils and teachers. Education Action Zones, specialist schools and beacon schools' initiatives all encourage schools to collaborate, to innovate and to be drivers of change.

In its National Strategy for Neighbourhood Renewal, the Social Exclusion Unit highlights the following ways in which local schools in deprived neighbourhoods can contribute towards neighbourhood renewal:

- *increasing 'Schools Plus' activities to help raise attainment in disadvantaged schools*
- *pupils in disadvantaged areas to have at least three hours of study support per week*
- *US style community schools – ensuring schools have better linkages with communities by employing local people as 'Community Learning Champions'*
- *make adult skills a priority by developing neighbourhood learning centres, offering 'first-rung' courses to attract people back to learning*
- *local IT learning centres – ensuring at least one publicly-accessible, community-based IT facility in each deprived neighbourhood by 2002; encouraging people to use them by employing local champions and offering user-friendly courses.*

The introduction of performance incentives and changes to pay structures are just one part of a package of reforms that will change the face of the teaching profession. The culture of schools will change as a range of different professionals come in to work alongside teachers and learners. Continual skills updating will be a feature of teachers' professional development. The new Leadership College based at Nottingham University will help to develop a new cadre of leaders for schools of the future, and network with international developments in school leadership. The General Teaching Council will be a watchdog and champion of professional standards in teaching.

Excerpt from Raising Aspirations in the 21st Century

'We need therefore secondary schools which:

- *have high expectations*
- *focus on individuals and their preferred learning styles*
- *challenge each pupil always to do better*
- *develop their strengths and contribute to a network of diverse provision across an area*

> ■ *are unashamed about excellence*
>
> ■ *remove barriers to learning wherever necessary*
>
> ■ *link young people to learning opportunities in other schools and outside the normal school day.'*

Successful schools operating in this way already exist, providing opportunities for learners undreamt of even ten years ago. But without exception the driver of these reforms is central and not local government. Funding is more and more tightly geared to implementation, with the LEA acting more and more as intermediary, passporting funds and negotiating with schools and other organisations on behalf of government.

CASE STUDY

Cranford Community College in West London is a community school with specialist language status, providing a rich learning resource for parents, students, staff who work at the college as well as teachers from local schools, local people, industry and business. The College has outstanding facilities for Information and Communication Technology, with an industry standard network that covers all areas of the college. Its Learning Resource Centre is open to students throughout the day for personal study, and before and after college hours for parents and adult users. As a Language Specialist college, the school offers an outstanding range and quality of modern foreign language courses, and links with schools and companies in all corners of the world. Its Language Excellence Centre provides a high quality training environment which is also available for local businesses and schools as a venue for staff development and business meetings, offering interactive whiteboard technology and video-conferencing facilities. The College has a number of very active links with industry, particularly British Airways and the British Airports Authority, British Telecom, Microsoft and Research Machines. It is also involved with a number of universities in curriculum research, providing a particularly rich career experience for staff in the college and in local primary schools in its openness to fresh ideas and forward thinking.

Schools and LEAs both complain that the volume and pace of reforms threaten to overwhelm their administrative capacity, and that the strong degree of regulation and the heavy handed approach to accountability attached to them can stifle the very creativity and responsiveness to local needs that they seek to address.

A recent report from the Government's Better Regulation Task Force, an independent group chaired by Lord Haskins that was set up in 1997 to advise government on improving the quality of its regulation, acknowledges these problems, but its recommendations go further than merely advising on ways to cut down on the paper work to lessen the burden on head teachers.

The 1998 Education Act with Fair Funding and the Code of Practice on LEA school relations has attempted to frame a new alliance between schools and LEAs. But the Task Force reported that it was 'struck by the confusion surrounding the role of LEAs', and said that no-one they spoke to, including representatives of LEAs, was able to clearly articulate their different roles.

It calls for a re-think of the statutory framework within which schools work, as each new Education Act has added new responsibilities without removing or clarifying what went before. It recommends that governing bodies should be reduced in size and that there should be clearer separation between their strategic and the headteacher's executive roles (Recommendations 2 & 3). Radical options for reform of school funding should be considered in the government's current three-year public spending review, with greater flexibility and delegation to successful schools and a move to three-year school budgets (Recommendation 6). And the government should 'review the role of LEAs in the funding of schools to simplify and avoid duplication, but should think carefully about the implications of excluding them from the process' (Recommendation 8). (*Red Tape Affecting Head Teachers,* April 2000.)

The government has responded with a commitment to cut bureaucracy, announcing that it will streamline the Standards Fund and cut by one third the number of documents and by one half the number of pages and paperwork sent automatically to schools by the DfEE in the next school year. The Code of Practice on LEA and school relations is to be revised and considerably shortened – down from 60 pages to no more than six – and, significantly, David Blunkett has said that the DETR Finance Green Paper, expected in the summer, will propose changes to the funding regime, including the introduction of three year funding settlements, and giving separate budgets for schools and local education authorities (*David Blunkett's speech to NAHT annual conference in Jersey, 1 February 2000*).

Missing from the debate about school funding and LEA/school responsibilities, however, is any reference to the LEA's place within local government. LEAs are not – or rather, should not be – stand alone authorities which operate in isolation from the rest of the council. Local government, like local education, is also going through a period of reform and transformation. Any review of the role of LEAs needs to examine reforms to local government and ask how far best value and new political structures might provide a new framework for LEA/school relationships that can support the needs of learners in the 21st century.

_____ Modern local government _____ and self managing schools

> 'There is no future in the old model of councils trying to plan and run most services ... Our modernising agenda is seeking nothing less than a radical refocusing of councils' traditional roles.'
>
> (1998 White Paper, *Modern Local Government, In Touch with the People*)

Self-managing schools are being encouraged to fly – to take on more and more responsibility, to develop ever wider professional networks and to become more and more accountable for the results they achieve.

Local education authorities, with their duty to promote high standards, have a duty to help schools to fly. LEA intervention in schools must be in 'inverse proportion to success'. The more successful LEAs are in promoting high standards, the less they should be involved in the daily concerns of schools. The judge and jury of a successful local authority will be the extent to which it can shed off its traditional LEA role.

But even the most successful schools are bound to their local authorities by locality, and by their shared concern for the needs of learners.

These are the two central strands of the modern authority's role in education – to help weaker schools to fly, and to help all schools connect with their localities on behalf of learners.

These strands are entirely congruent with the agenda for modern local government which puts community leadership at the heart of the role of modern local authorities.

The first legislation to implement these reforms came into force in April, with a duty on councils to secure best value in the provision of services and to undertake fundamental performance reviews of all of their services over a five year period. These reviews must challenge how and why a service is being provided, compare the service with the performance that others are achieving, consult with local taxpayers, service users and the wider business community on how the service can be improved, and embrace fair competition as a means of securing efficient and effective services. Councils must prepare annual performance plans, bringing together the outcomes of their reviews, setting new targets and reporting back on progress. The reviews will be inspected, and Ministers have the power to intervene when services fall below acceptable standards.

In education, the early introduction of a 'best value' regime – through target-setting, education development planning, inspection and intervention – is already proving a significant lever for change. There is more focus on priorities for raising standards, better planning to meet targets and a clearer delineation of schools and LEA responsibilities. Where LEA support for school improvement is weak, external intervention is leading to the development of new strategic partnerships for strategic planning and for the delivery of services. Under best value, these are all options that any authority might decide to pursue as a result of their best value reviews.

CASE STUDY

In Leicester City Council a Partnership Board has been established to add strategic drive to the implementation of the modernisation agenda and to build linkages and feedback between schools, communities and the council. The Partnership Board is chaired by Professor David Hopkins, professor of education at Nottingham University. Members include the leader of the council, chair of the council's education committee, two opposition councillors and a headteacher, as well as external partners at a very senior level and with acknowledged standing in their respective fields across the public, private and voluntary sectors. The Board will oversee a new development support agency which will work closely with schools to help them exchange information, share good practice and provide mutual challenge and support.

Outsourcing all or part of the education service does not divorce the authority from its schools, but could gain better value for money for those services, and frees up the authority to focus on its core strategic role of championing local educational needs. Inviting new partners in to manage schools does not divorce those schools from the public sector, but can provide new opportunities for learners as new approaches are brought in to tackle what appear to be intractable problems, and new partnership boards that are established to support the local authority's strategic management of education can provide a stimulus and dynamic to corporate thinking, and spur the development of learning networks. In Islington, where Cambridge Education Associates has been contracted to run the Borough's education services, the process of letting and monitoring the contract has required detailed and on-going scrutiny of every aspect of the service and its value to local stakeholders. In Surrey, the County Council awarded a contract to 3 Es Enterprises Ltd, a wholly owned subsidiary of the Kingshurst City Technology College, to provide a fresh start for the failing Kings Manor School and a secure future for secondary pupils within its catchment area. The school was closed and re-opened as a new non-denominational voluntary aided school, Kings College. Responsibility for its success lies with the school's governing body and headteacher, working with the education authority – but both the school and the authority gain from 3Es' expertise and track record in raising school standards and the private sector investment it can bring in to enhance the school buildings.

The next stage of local government reform, the Local Government (Organisation and Standards) Bill, is the necessary corollary to best value. The emphasis in this bill is on leadership and governance and the role that local government can play in developing a strong civic society.

The new power of community well-being will enable local authorities to engage in partnership arrangements with other bodies and organisations that operate locally for any purpose which supports their function, including the function of promoting the economic, social and environmental well-being of the area. The powers will provide scope for pooling or sharing of resources, accommodation, IT and staff, and will encourage the delegation of responsibility for decisions within an agreed framework or plan.

Strategies to meet local educational needs drawn up under the power of community initiative would place the needs of learners first. Providers should be the best organisations to meet needs. In education this could mean a mixture of public, private and voluntary sector institutions all making a contribution towards meeting needs. Indeed, the more we expect of schools, and the tougher the targets they have to meet, the more they will need to collaborate with a range of different 'experts' and organisations to meet the needs of learners.

These powers give local authorities the leverage to work with the ever-widening range of education providers to agree a comprehensive strategy for learning in local communities. The more diverse educational service provision becomes, the more important it is that everyone involved subscribes to a set of core values that underpin their work. In their community leadership role, local authorities can help to set the core values that place the needs of learners in their localities first, and work with partners to agree the strategies that are needed to ensure that national and local priorities are addressed.

In a recent seminar Professor Brian Caldwell suggested the following core values for a world class education system:

- *choice: the right of parents and students to schools that meet their needs and aspirations*
- *equity: to provide assurance that students with similar needs and aspirations will be treated in the same manner in the course of their education*
- *access: to ensure that all students will have an education that matches their needs and aspirations*
- *efficiency: to optimise outcomes given the resources available*
- *economic growth: to regenerate resources that are adequate to the task*
- *harmony: to remedy the current fragmentation of commitment and effort in support of schools*

('Putting the public good back into public education', Brian Caldwell, professor and dean of education at the University of Melbourne, May 2000).

Networks like these, led by a strong strategic partnerships, already exist. Early Years Education and Childcare Strategies and the Sure Start initiative both illustrate this multi-strand approach to the planning and delivery of services for young children and their families. They illustrate how diversity in provision can be a positive and even an essential component of meeting diverse needs, rather than a threat to individual service providers.

CASE STUDY

Pyramids of schools (Northumberland)

Within Northumberland, 16 pyramids of schools provide education for 4 to 18 year olds. Each of the high schools is responsible for community education in the community served by the pyramid.

The Coquet Pyramid includes an Early Excellence Centre. It serves a rural area with small centres of population and significant social and economic deprivation following the decline of local mining and fishing industries.

The Early Years Excellence Centre brings together education, welfare and family support services, combining an integrated network and a multi-disciplinary approach throughout the locality. Improved career and training opportunities for everyone involved with early years – including young parents, school students and the unemployed – is a key feature of the Centre's work.

> It has a Steering Group made up of representatives of all the service providers (private and public) – education, health, social services, child minders, as well as headteachers, parents, elected members, NTEC, higher education, the chair of the Coquet Pyramid.
>
> The Coquet Early Excellence Centre, described above, draws its funding from 12 different sources: Rural Development Commission; DfEE; New Opportunities Fund; Health Action Zone; SRB; Energi; LEA; Northumberland TEC; Private Industry; Charitable Trusts; Fees; Local Authorities.

The Bill also makes provisions for new political management structures, separating the executive and scrutiny roles of elected members, and introducing elected mayors and possibly even elected heads of service into authorities. These new political structures can help to bring education into the corporate centre of local government, leading to more integrated planning of community strategies for lifelong learning. Scrutiny committees can focus their attention on outcomes for learners, and councillors in their representative role can trawl widely in their communities for evidence of what is happening and of what matters to local people. The development of influential neighbourhood forums can help to give local people a real say, and a shared responsibility, in developments that effect them. And , as the experience of mayors in cities such as Barcelona and Bonn has shown, an elected mayor can provide a focus for community leadership as a visible figure, providing a bridge to link disparate groups together and spearheading partnerships for regeneration. In education, which is such a high priority, a city mayor who could use the influence of office and the legitimacy of the mayor's elected status to raise aspiration and draw in support and resources to raise standards, would confer real legitimacy on local government and help to force the pace of decentralisation.

CASE STUDY

> A scrutiny committee established in Lewisham to review the Borough's GCSE results made a significant impact on the attitudes of elected members. The process of facing difficult issues – the generally poor standards of performance at GCSE level and the reasons behind it – helped to challenge their own thinking about their role in the authority, moving from a traditional stance of defending services on behalf of local government, to one of bringing constructive criticism of services on behalf of local people.

All of these developments place the needs of local people first. The desire to assert a stronger local identity, evidenced through moves to regional government in Scotland, Wales and England, seems to grow stronger as we become more global. Writing in the *Local Government Chronicle* (7 April 2000) Sir Michael Lyons, Chief Executive, Birmingham City Council, described this paradox

> 'in an era of the international citizen, it seems everyone wants to be an individual',

and the challenge this presents for public services

> 'where standardisation and consistency have long been regarded as key components of a fair system of rationing scarce public resources.'

Strong local government, with a reach that extends down into the smallest communities, but also outwards into regional and national institutions, can help to facilitate the networks that will enable self managing schools to meet the needs of local learners, and provide the strategic leadership and vision that is needed to ensure that plurality in education becomes a strength – a positive response to local needs – and not a threat to cohesion.

'Beyond the self managing school' – developing new learning networks

Schools of the future must have the leadership and the capacity to determine and manage their own destinies, anticipate and understand the changing needs of stakeholders and continuously adapt their practice to develop new educational models that work. They also need to be able to draw in considerable extra resources to supplement their statutory funding and build the networks that can enable them to meet the diverse needs of their learning communities.

Self managing schools are largely autonomous organisations, linked to their LEAs, but not necessarily linked to each other. Government initiatives that tie additional funding to collaboration are beginning to challenge the culture of competition and isolation that so marked the early stages of educational reforms, and they also underline the key strategic role that LEAs have to play in supporting effective networks. But current school governance and funding regimes militate against the kind of collaboration that can bring about a real change in the culture of schools and really open up opportunities for learners.

If there is to be a step change in education, educational institutions of the future will need to have the powers to group into self-managed networks that can consolidate key strategic decisions about direction, values, strategies and resources, whilst local authorities focus on their core role in connecting schools to their localities and building partnerships for educational success.

Operating within self-managed learning networks, schools would collaborate with and learn from each other in the transformation and continuous improvement process, leverage economies of scale, and raise additional funding to enhance their core services.

The DETR reforms set out the role the local authority would play. Exercising the new power of community initiative, local government would identify local needs, set local performance indicators, agree targets, lever in funds and support strategic partnerships to provide services on behalf of local people. It would champion equality and fairness in the system, and challenge providers to produce better outcomes. Within this framework, schools within self-managing learning networks, together with other organisations, would in effect be commissioned by local authorities to deliver services on behalf of local people.

To move from a pattern of autonomous institutions working within limited networks, to more structured, more focused and more powerful self-managing learning networks, new incentives will be needed to motivate schools and other educational institutes to work together.

In the initial stages, significant new funding will need to be made available to enable networks to make real changes to operational structures, and it will need to be sufficiently flexible to enable learners to access opportunity across a range of institutions – including, possibly, private and voluntary sector institutions – in the networks. Clear goals will need to be set to establish the prerequisites for moving from one governance status to the next. For example, a specified new governance model, clear development plans and a range of targets encompassing pupil performance and new management goals.

As schools and networks meet the criteria established at these thresholds, they could be granted new freedoms and funding entitlements, related to the better value that they are demonstrating in their performance statistics. At their most basic level, self-governing learning networks might share and develop expertise in curriculum development and experiment with new management and leadership systems appropriate to 21st century new learning models. Those that significantly exceeded performance criteria could take on significant additional responsibilities, and be commissioned to plan and provide a range of services to meet the wider educational needs of their localities.

Funding for learning networks – additional to schools formula funding – could be drawn from a range of sources, for example from SRB funding, DETR New Deal for Community funds, Health Authority initiatives, the Learning and Skills Council and DfEE grants for national initiatives, as well as from commercial partnerships the networks enter into, and from their own fundraising efforts. Some funding might be channelled via local authorities and the community learning strategy, and some might be paid directly to the networks.

Customer focused organisations will be needed to provide high value added services to the learning networks at competitive and affordable costs. As the majority of these services are based in LEAs, consideration should be given to ways of outsourcing them, either through local authority strategic partnerships with private sector providers, or by privatising them. This would put these services on a more commercial and competitive footing and place authorities in a stronger position to challenge their quality and relevance for stakeholders.

In order to enable, regulate and integrate these new self managed organisations an appropriate allocation of responsibilities and powers will have to be agreed between the DfEE, local authorities and other relevant bodies such as the Regional Development Agencies to ensure that both national education standards and local community goals are exceeded. These responsibilities could include:

- licensing of school operators (appropriate to levels of freedoms and responsibilities given to the learning networks. In the most advanced cases, this would include obligations to supply places and a duty to integrate)
- monitoring and counselling of the operators of educational institutions
- power to downgrade the governance status in the event of performance decline
- intervention in cases of sustained under performance against minimum national standards
- provision of strategic service support in areas beyond reasonable commercial capacity (e.g. for insurable events).

In reviewing a new balance of powers and responsibilities between central government, local authorities and other relevant bodies, consideration should be given as to whether the local authority's new power of community initiative should be strengthened to become a duty, with a commensurate duty on other public bodies – or bodies that receive public funds – to cooperate. Inherent in the current framework there are real tensions between 'choice and diversity' and equity. These tensions would be significantly reduced if self managing learning institutions were required to subscribe to the core values and the wider social programmes of the locality as a condition of their licence.

External inspection and intervention strategies would provide a failsafe for local communities, and for learning institutions, where local authorities fail to operate as effective community leaders. But where local authorities play a strong role and give a real lead in building effective partnerships in education, they could be rewarded with additional funding, or with the power to raise additional funding, to support their work.

New learning networks would begin to develop a picture of what future models of local education might look like. Some networks may be locally based, others based on communities of interest or shared expertise. They may incorporate state and independent schools, or schools and other institutions that can provide learning opportunities. In all cases, schools would be connected to their localities, but draw strength from their networks to support their work in meeting the needs of learners. And in all cases, decisions about who provides education and how it would be driven by the needs of learners and not by the needs of producers.

In a rural area, schools may operate as a network of local learning centres, linked to a hub. New patterns of schooling might develop, mixing home learning with school attendance and including learners of all ages, and staff would be expert in distance learning methods. In an inner city, a learning network may integrate public and private institutions to afford staff and learners the widest possible opportunities relevant to their diverse needs, and at the same time, provide the services that support the pastoral care of students and their families.

CASE STUDY

In Somerset, the County Council has already embarked on an exercise to encourage new learning networks to develop. Somerset Education aims to work in partnership to raise achievement, promote lifelong learning and develop effective learning communities. In the Autumn of 1999 it published a consultation document setting out a strategic vision for the way that learning could be organised in the future. *Learning in Somerset, Looking Forward 2000 to 2020* framed its objectives in the context of changing employment patterns and the impact of new technology:

'The demands of the 21st Century and the potential of new technology provide an opportunity to re-think how education is organised and how access to it is provided in a rural county.'

The document sets out proposals for change under eight key ideas (the figure in brackets indicates the percentage of consultees in favour of the proposals):

1 Encourage staff in schools and other learning establishments to work more closely together. (85 per cent)

2 Establish geographically-based Community Learning Areas, where learning providers would share responsibility for planning, delivering and managing learning programmes. (65 per cent)

3 Establish pilot governing bodies responsible for management, resources and service delivery for all learning establishments within the 'Community Learning Area'. (37 per cent – with 33 per cent disagreeing and 30 per cent expressing no preference)

4 Increase the use of educational facilities to provide all year round learning. (81 per cent)

5 Establish a purpose built 'Community Learning Centre' to cater for learners of all ages and act as a base for multi agency work. (55 per cent, with the remaining 45 per cent equally split between disagreement and no option)

6 Review the traditional school year and day. (63 per cent)

7 Pilot alternative ways of learning, with learners involved in determining their own learning and support needs. (76 per cent)

8 Provide further learning opportunities available to, and accessible by, everyone through computer technology. (79 per cent).

The authority has now embarked on series of pilot projects and further research to test these ideas.

Somerset's consultation exercise demonstrated considerable support for radical change in the way that education is structured and delivered. A government commitment to funding a series of new learning networks would require a one-off cost but for long-term gain, as most of the mechanisms for new models of local education are already in place, or soon will be once the DETR legislation is enacted.

The DETR reforms require a substantial cultural shift in the way that local government operates. It is a challenge that is more likely to be embraced if elected members and other community leaders believe that, through the reforms, they will be able to help to shape the future of local education in a way that will make a real difference to their communities. Healthy families, an active citizenry, a confident and well qualified work-force feeding in to the local economy are all nurtured by cradle to grave lifelong learning opportunities. If local government has any role in local communities, then education must be a part of that role.

Working to local community learning strategies, diverse learning networks would draw strength from partnership working, an empowered teaching profession, and the strategic leadership of modern local government.

Future models of local education – executive summary

Operating within a strong, centrally-determined framework, self managing schools are being encouraged to fly – to determine and manage their own destinies, to develop ever wider professional networks, and to become more and more accountable for the results they achieve.

But as the LEA's traditional role in education diminishes, local government's core strategic role in connecting schools to their localities and building partnerships for educational success becomes even more important.

Under the new power of community initiative, local authorities will have the leverage to work with education providers and other organisations that can support their work to agree a comprehensive strategy for learning that embraces national standards and local community goals. Diversity would become a strength and not a threat to cohesion, as a mixture of public, private and voluntary sector institutions are drawn in to the strategy – as is happening already in early years education and childcare – to meet local needs. In this new commissioning role, local authorities would take a more robust position on behalf of learners – identifying local needs, agreeing local targets that complement national goals, levering in additional funds for education, supporting strategic partnerships for delivery, and challenging outcomes.

To make this transition towards a more strategic role for local government, consideration should be given to the following:

- encouraging the outsourcing of local authority back-office functions to put them on a more commercial and competitive footing, and to place authorities in a stronger position to challenge their quality and relevance for stakeholders

- providing incentives to encourage schools and other educational institutions to group together within self-managed learning networks that can consolidate key strategic decisions about directions, values, strategies and resources; with potential for networks to gain new freedoms and funding entitlements as they demonstrate better value in their agreeing a new allocation of appropriate responsibilities and powers between the DfEE, local authorities, other relevant bodies (e.g. RDAs) to ensure that both national standards and local community goals are exceeded; including consideration of whether the new power of community initiative should become a duty, with a commensurate duty on other public bodies – or bodies that receive public funds – to cooperate.

Rather than being marginalised by the increasing freedoms being given to self-managing learning institutions, local authorities have a real opportunity to help shape the future of local education. Working to local community learning strategies, diverse learning networks would draw strength from partnership working, an empowered teaching profession and the strategic leadership of modern local government.

———— A golden era for school leadership ————

Recognition of the importance of education to the wellbeing of the nation, with at least nine exciting domains for innovation, matched by a challenge to abandon what gets in the way, surely heralds a golden era for school leadership. This is especially the case with a vision as expansive as that from the Vision 2020 conference theme: One World, One School – the Globalisation of Lifelong Learning. The ninth domain is a salutary reminder that boundary spanning on a global scale may be a great deal easier than boundary spanning at the local level. We must do both and do them well if expectations for world-class schools are to be realised.

References

Audit Commission (1999) *Lessons in Teamwork*

Barber, M. (1996) *The Learning Game*, London: Victor Gollancz

Barber, M. (2000) Learning Environment in 2005, response to a question from a speech given in Washington DC on 30 May 2000 and reported on DfEE website: www.dfee.gov.uk

Bennis, W. and Bierderman, P. (1998) *Organizing Genius*, London: Nicholas Brealey

Blanchard, K., Oncken, Jr., Burrows, H. (1990) *The One Minute Manager Meets the Monkey*, London: Collins

Blanchard, K., Zigarmi, D. and Zigarmi, P. (1987) *Leadership and the One Minute Manager*, London: Collins

Bowring-Carr, C. and West-Burnham, J. (1997) *Effective Learning in Schools*, London: Pitman

Caldwell, B. (2000) *Scenarios for Leadership and Abandonment in the Transformation of Schools*, key-note address at the 13th International Congress for School Effectiveness and Improvement on the theme 'Global Networking for Quality Education', Hong Kong Institute of Education, Hong Kong, 8 January 2000

Caldwell, B. and Spinks, J. (1998) *Beyond the Self-Managing School*, London: Falmer

Covey, S. (1992) *The Seven Habits of Highly Effective People*, London: Simon & Schuster

Covey, S. and Merrill, A. (1994) *First Things First*, London: Simon & Schuster

Davies, B. and Ellison, L. (1997) *School Leadership for the 21st Century*, London: Routledge

Davies, B. and Ellison, L. (1999) *Strategic Direction and Development of the School*, London: Routledge

de Bono, E. (1990) *Six Thinking Hats*, London: Penguin

de Bono, E. (2000) *New Thinking for the New Millennium*, London: Penguin

Drucker, P. (1999) *Management Challenges for the 21st Century*, London: Butterworth-Heinemann

East Midlands Electricity, (1995) Quality Improvement Tools, East Midlands Electricity

Fitz-Gibbon, C. (1995) *Monitoring Education: Quality, Indicators and Effectiveness*, London: Cassell

Gardner, H. (1993) *The Unschooled Mind*, London: Fontana

Gardner, H. (1995) *Leading Minds*, New York: Basic Books

Gates, W. (1995) *The Road Ahead*, London: Viking

Gates, W. (2000) *Business @ the Speed of Thought*, London: Penguin

Goldratt, E. (1990) *The Theory of Constraints*, Mass: North River Press

Goldratt, E. (1994) *It's Not Luck*, London: Gower

Goldratt, E. and Cox, J. (1984) *The Goal*, London: Gower

Goleman, D. (1996) *Emotional Intelligence*, London: Bloomsbury

Groves, M. (1999) *Growing Families of Schools*, London: TC Trust

Handy, C. (1995) *The Empty Raincoat*, London: Arrow

Hargreaves, D. (1998) *The Role of Teachers in the Knowledge Society*, London: Demos

Hay Mcber (1999) *Research into Highly Effective Heads*, Powerpoint presentation, November 1999

Hay Mcber (2000) *A Model of Teacher Effectiveness*, DfEE website: www.dfee.gov.uk/teachingreforms/mcber

Jesson, D. (2000) *Value Added in Specialist Schools*, Technology Colleges Trust

Johnson, M. (ed.) (2000) *Education Futures*, London: RSA/Design Council

Kerry, T. (2000), Working Paper No. 40, *Surviving the Future: Changing Education in a Changing World*, University of Lincolnshire and Humberside

Knight, B. (1993) *Financial Management for Schools*, London: Heinemann

Oracle, (2000) Toolkit, Oracle Website: www.think.com

Peters, T. (1988) *Thriving on Chaos*, London: Macmillan

Peters, T. (1997) *The Circle of Innovation*, London: Hodder and Stoughton

Peters, T. and Austin, N. (1985) *A Passion for Excellence*, New York: Random House

Peters, T. and Waterman, R. (1982) *In Search of Excellence*, New York: Harper and Row

Reynolds, D. and Cuttance, P. (1992) *School Effectiveness*, London: Cassell

Roberts, W. (1989) *Leadership Secrets of Attila the Hun*, London: Bantam

Rutter, M. et al. (1979) *Fifteen Thousand Hours*, London: Open Books

Seltzer, K. and Bentley, T. (1999) *The Creative Age*, London: Demos

TC Trust, (1999) Standards Audit

Teacher Training Agency (1998) Leadership Programme for Serving Heads

Teacher Training Agency (1998) National Standards for Headteachers

Thomas, A. (1998) *Educating Children at Home*, London: Cassell

Tooley, J. and Howes, A. (1999) *The Seven Habits of Highly Effective Schools*, London: TC Trust

Wheatley, M. (1992) *Leadership and the New Science*, San Francisco: Berrett-Koehler

References used for the preparation of *Future Models of Local Education*:

Accountability and Choice in Schooling, Mike Feintuck, Open University Press, ISBN 0 335 15730 0

The Annual Report of Her Majesty's Chief Inspector of Schools 1998/99, Office for Standards in Education, ISBN 0 10 556644 6

Best value in education, a practical guide, Paul Corrigan, Published by the New Local Government Network for Initial Educational Personnel, ISBN 0 9534 903 8 6

Beyond the Self-Managing School, Brain J. Caldwell and Jim M. Spinks, Falmer Press, ISBN 0 7507 0448 9

Consorting and Collaborating in the Education Marketplace, Ed. David Bridges and Chris Husbands, Falmer Press, ISBN 0 7507 0450 0

Creative Professionalism: The role of teachers in the knowledge society, David Hargreaves, Demos 1998, ISBN 1 898309 79 5

Fairer Funding: Proposals for a national funding entitlement for schools, Peter Downs OBE, Secondary Heads Association, January 2000, ISBN 0 906916 54 2

Funding for schools has become a total lottery says NAHT, National Association of Head Teachers Press Release, statistics on disparities of funding between one local education authority and another dated 25 November 1999

Held in trust, the LEA of the future, Audit Commission, ISBN 1 86240 133 0

Learning Beyond the Classroom: Education for a changing world, Tom Bentley, Demos, ISBN 0 415 18259 X

The Learning Game: Arguments for an education revolution, Michael Barber, Victor Gollancz, ISBN 0 575 06364 5

Modern Local Government, In Touch With the People, DETR White Paper, 1998 ISBN 0 10 140142 6

More spending power for schools and less red tape – Blunkett, DfEE Press Release, Speech to NAHT annual conference in Jersey, 1 February 2000

The Mosaic of Learning: Schools and Teachers for the Next Century, Demos, ISBN 1 898 309 45 0

National Strategy for Neighbourhood Renewal: a framework for consultation, Report by the Social Exclusion Unit, April 2000, Cabinet Office

Part of the solution, Perspectives on the future educational role of the local authority, Local Government Association, ISBN 1 84049 129 9

Raising Aspirations in the 21st Century, A speech by the Rt Hon David Blunkett MP, Secretary of State for Education and Employment, 6 January 2000, DfEE Publications

Red Tape Affecting Head Teachers, Better Regulation Task Force, April 2000, Cabinet Office, ISBN 0 7115 0396 6

What a difference a mayor makes, Karen Day, Published by the New Local Government Network, ISBN 0 9534 903 7 8

Index